D1104844

A Handbook for
the Ballet Accompanist

A HANDBOOK FOR THE BALLET ACCOMPANIST

Gerald R. Lishka

WITHDRAWN

INDIANA UNIVERSITY PRESS

Bloomington & London

Copyright © 1979 by Gerald R. Lishka

All rights reserved

No part of this book may be reproduced or utilized in any form or by any
means, electronic or mechanical, including photocopying and recording,
or by any information storage and retrieval system, without permission
in writing from the publisher. The Association of American University
Presses' Resolution on Permissions constitutes the only exception to this
prohibition.

Manufactured in the United States of America

Library of Congress Cataloging in Publication Data

Lishka, Gerald R., 1949-
    A handbook for the ballet accompanist.

    Includes index.
    1. Musical accompaniment.   2. Ballet dance
music.   3. Piano—Instruction and study.
I. Title.
MT950.L7   786.3'04'1   78-2051
ISBN 0-253-32704-0 1 2 3 4 5 83 82 81 80 79

ERFORMING ARTS LIBRARY

MT
950
.L7

To Ben and Betty Johnston, with
deepest gratitude for their enduring
friendship, support, and selfless love.

79 3182

Contents

Contents

Preface

The purpose of this book is to advise and instruct pianists in the art of
ballet accompaniment. It discusses the many and varied facets of accompanying for ballet classes and familiarizes the pianist with the
general procedure and format observed in ballet studios. It defines and
discusses, from the standpoint of the accompanist, much of the basic,
essential ballet terminology, and places it in a perspective which is
relevant and practical for the pianist in terms of his function in the
ballet studio. Many suggestions and guidelines are given to the pianist
to aid him in the selection, preparation, arrangement, and appropriate
use of piano literature potentially suitable for accompanying ballet
classes. The numerous problems which inevitably arise for the ballet
accompanist are discussed in detail, and many helpful hints and solutions are offered which will spare him from unnecessary mistakes,
wasted time and energy, and potential embarrassment.

The pianist will be aided in acquiring a firm grasp on the practical
concepts and problems with which the ballet accompanist must deal.
Many of these problems are difficult to articulate, in that ballet accompanying is to a degree an instinctive art (in this way like any artistic skill
which requires native talent). But the real mastery of any artistic discipline demands conscious control and firm objective knowledge. It is
our aim to supply that knowledge here.

This book is not intended to be an exhaustive ballet textbook or
dictionary, nor does it attempt to approach being a complete syllabus of
music literature for use in the ballet class. It does, however, point the
pianist in the direction which will enable him to orient himself in this

challenging field. Accompanying the ballet, and doing it well, is a unique skill which requires a great deal of experience, a resourceful and flexible musical imagination, and a special sensitivity to dance movements. This experience and sensitivity must be developed chiefly in an applied context—in the ballet studio. It would be extremely difficult for the ordinary pianist to imagine all of the problems which are inherent in dance accompaniment. Generally, and often of necessity, the dancer hears and interprets music differently than the trained musician does. The dance accompanist must learn to empathize with the physical and mental processes whereby the dancer relates music to the art of dance.

Succinctly stated, the challenge of the dance accompanist is this: to provide the quality of musical support and inspiration which is absolutely necessary for the dancer, while maintaining at the same time his own sense of musical individuality and integrity; to cooperate in a workable relationship that will be personally and artistically fulfilling to both the dancer and to the musician.

I wish to express here a special thank you to Merritt Lishka, for her knowledge and patience in assisting me with the arrangement, content, and definition of ballet steps and terminology in this book.

A Handbook for
the Ballet Accompanist

The Ballet Class

The Ballet Studio

The facilities of individual dance studios vary greatly. One finds a drastically wide range in such factors as availability and quality of lighting, ventilation, studio dimensions, and acoustical traits. The enrollment of a dance class may range from a mere handful up to thirty, forty, or even a hundred or more dancers. The length of classes may be, forty-five to sixty minutes or two or even three hours. The size of the dance studio may be comparable to the dimensions of an average family living room, or it may measure perhaps eighty by one hundred fifty feet. One encounters all sizes, conditions, and makes of pianos, from the most decrepit spinet to the finest concert grand. Depending on where one accompanies, the caliber of dancers and dance instructors varies widely, from the most demanding, fastidious, and professional artists to the rankest amateurs.

In most ballet studios there are horizontal barres made of wood or metal, which are spaced along the walls, sometimes at varying heights from the floor. These provide support and balance to the dancers while they are doing their barre exercises. Many studios feature large mirrors on one or more of the walls. Dance floors are usually wood (which is the best material), but sometimes linoleum tile is used. Some of the variable factors mentioned above may directly affect the accompanist, and all influence his style of accompanying.

Prerecorded Music

Good accompanists are more than an asset to the ballet class—they are practically indispensable. If the class does not have the advantage of an accompanist, there are two alternatives, neither of which is very desirable. The instructor may elect to teach the class without music. To say the least, this is a very frustrating and undesirable situation. Aside from being totally uninspiring for both the students and the instructor, such an environment does nothing to develop or expand the musicality of the dancers. The instructor is left to his own resources, such as singing, clapping his hands or snapping his fingers, and stamping on the floor. The only result is an exhausted instructor with sore hands and a raw throat.

As a second alternative, the instructor may elect to employ some type of prerecorded music, using either a record player or a tape machine. Although prerecorded music is far better than no music at all, it has many drawbacks. First, it imposes severe limitations on the creative capabilities and spontaneity of the instructor. It is a limited and inflexible source from which to draw. Such inherent drawbacks are heightened by the fact that the same recordings are often used over and over again, possibly for a very long period of time. Second, the necessity of having to employ prerecorded music must unquestionably disrupt the flow, momentum, and spontaneity of the dance class. After teaching a particular dance combination to a class, the instructor must then grope and fumble for a suitable and appropriate musical selection. This entails locating the exact spot on a tape or pinpointing a particular groove on a record, which not only consumes a great deal of time but is highly disruptive to a continuous train of thought.

Although any ballet class will reflect a certain format and order which is fairly universal (and which will be fully discussed later), there remains ample opportunity for the instructor to modify and to improvise upon the established routines. This may be done in order to devote more time to specific weaknesses of the dancers, to address certain individual needs, or to emphasize a particular point in that class. With prerecorded music, the instructor is faced with locating suitable music for each of these situations, which is a nuisance. It is also time consuming, as well as inadequate for dealing with impromptu situations which arise during class, if the instructor wishes to select and prepare music before class. The situations outlined above make for a very rigid class, and if unforeseen problems arise, the preestablished routine is disrupted.

Finally, using prerecorded music means that the tempo of any particular dance combination is established and unalterable. Given the variance in many factors—the abilities of the dancers, the technical difficulty of any given step, the condition of the dancers' muscles—the inflexibility of prerecorded music is an irksome problem and greatly diminishes the possibilities that can be explored during the dance class.

The answer is a live accompanist (provided he is a good one). The presence of an accompanist who is attentive, responsive, and experienced will alleviate all such difficulties and make life in the studio much easier for both instructor and students.

The Attitude of the Accompanist

The accompanist is an important and vital influence in the ballet studio. His effect is keenly felt. He may greatly inspire a dance class, or he may totally neutralize and destroy its momentum, depending on his individual ability, experience, sensitivity, and temperament. Both the instructor and the dance students, if they have any musical sensitivity at all, will be very much aware of the accompanist, and of his frame of mind, as it is projected through his accompanying. It is therefore essential that the accompanist make a real effort to maintain and project a buoyant, healthy, and interested attitude toward the class. He may successfully achieve this in a number of ways: by improvising often, summoning from his own creativity new and fresh musical ideas; by using a wide variety of repertory, while searching regularly for new music of contrasting styles, so that his playing does not become hackneyed and stale; and by maintaining an active interest in the actual mechanics of the ballet class, remaining attentive and alert to the dialogue and to the corrections.

The Accompanist as Music Educator

Whether or not he is consciously aware of it, one of the primary functions of the accompanist who plays for ballet classes day after day is that of music educator. Quite often, the music which the accompanist plays in the dance studio is one of the primary sources, if not the only source, of serious music literature to which the dance student is exposed. Those dance students who have the opportunity to study music theory or literature, or to study a musical instrument along with their dance training, are very fortunate. They are bound to be better artists as a result of this exposure and experience. Since many dancers do not have such an opportunity, their musical outlooks and tastes frequently suffer severely. The accompanist is often an individual to whom dancers are exposed regularly, over a long period of time. The accompanist's training, musical taste, and experience are potentially an excellent source of musical knowledge and exposure for the dance students, not to mention the instructor.

Although there is definitely much piano music which is unsuitable for the dance class, the body of piano literature on which the pianist may draw is practically infinite. The pianist who can readily improvise is even less limited, for obvious reasons, and the pianist who possesses some knowledge of vocal and operatic literature will have yet another immense source of material. The ballet accompanist will find that it is a real challenge to avoid having his playing become stale, either to himself and to the dancers. He should continually be expanding his own dance repertory—for his sake, and for the sake of the classes for which he accompanies. In this way, he will be introducing and familiarizing the dancers with more and more kinds of music literature. Not only will this be an intellectual challenge and stimulus to the dancers, but it will help to prepare them for the great variety of music to which they will be exposed while dancing professionally. For those dance students who intend at some point during their careers to become dance teachers themselves, such exposure will also be invaluable.

Knowing Ballet Terminology

The inexperienced ballet accompanist need not be intimidated by the fact that he may be relatively or even totally unfamiliar with the terminology of ballet. There are many dance dictionaries available, if he wishes to study them, such as the *Technical Manual and Dictionary of Classical Ballet,* by Gail Grant (New York: Dover Publications, 1967). Knowing the names of the various dance steps and having an idea of the mechanics involved will obviously be helpful and will make the accompanist more at ease in the ballet studio. Such knowledge may be gained gradually as the accompanist acquires more experience. However, the essential matter of concern for the new dance accompanist is to observe carefully the motions and movements of the dancers, sensitizing himself to their maneuvers. Generally, the dance instructor will demonstrate at least part of any dance combination to the students before they attempt to do it, and after a little experience the accompanist will be able to grasp the essential idea behind the step and will grow more adept at selecting music which is suitable in feeling and tempo. Understanding dance instructors will assist the accompanist by indicating in some way the kind of music they would like to have. They may at least suggest a suitable time signature, for instance, a "broad ¾," a "lively waltz," or a "sharp ²⁄₄."

Indeed, it would be little problem for the experienced ballet accompanist to function in a dance class in which the language spoken was totally foreign to him. By observing the instructor demonstrate, he could easily ascertain all that he needed to know. Such an accompanist would have developed the essential ability to empathize with the dancers' movements. Ballet is an art which is fairly universal in its basic nature. And regardless of where the ballet class is being given, whether in the United States, in Russia, or in Brazil, the terminology of the ballet is always in French. The general ballet vocabulary is very stable: a plié is always a plié, a tendu is always a tendu. Of course, the pianist who understands ballet terminology is in a more secure position than one who does not.

Understanding the Instructor

The accompanist should be advised that the instructor may occasionally and unintentionally mislead him, while attempting in good faith to describe the kind of music he would like for a particular dance step. The instructor may request a piece of music with a certain feeling or a specific tempo. For example, he may ask for a "lively three" (¾). The pianist may have a piece of music that, rather than being in a ¾ meter, is in a ⁶⁄₈ meter and which, in this particular case, would do quite well. It will all depend on the specific quality and feeling of the piece of music in question. When a dance instructor asks for a piece of music in ²⁄₄ time, he often has in mind a very bright duple meter; a ⁴⁄₄ meter might be just as suitable, perhaps even a ⁶⁄₈. In other words, the dance accompanist will often find that a dance teacher, in articulating his feelings about music, does so somewhat differently from the manner in which a formally trained musician might express himself. While this sometimes leads to confusion and misunderstanding, it need not become a serious problem. With experience the dance accompanist learns to understand easily what is being required of him and exercises a degree of tolerance toward the instructor in such situations. As the accompanist grows to know more intimately those with whom he is working, he can of course empathize more readily with them.

There are many instances, however, in which the accompanist must furnish exactly what is asked of him, for instance, a "bright mazurka" or a "stately polonaise." Dance instructors vary drastically in their musical tastes and preferences. Many teachers are extremely knowledgeable and articulate, musically. Others will accept just about anything. Some will be maddeningly insistent in terms of just exactly what kind of music they want from the accompanist. Occasionally a dance instructor may reject a piece of music that the dance accompanist is using, simply because it does not strike his fancy or suit his whim. The accompanist must learn not to take such things personally, which is sometimes difficult to do. Often, the accompanist has enormous freedom of choice in selecting music for a particular step; as long as he plays his choice well and communicates the appropriate feeling, the necessary requirement is met. If a dance teacher indicates merely a "broad adagio," for instance, the accompanist might select a slow, flowing ¾, ⁴⁄₄, ¹²⁄₈ or whatever, as long as it supports and reinforces the movements of the dancers.

Asking When in Doubt

Occasionally even an excellent accompanist will have difficulty in immediately grasping an idea that the dance instructor is conveying to the class. From time to time he may find himself at somewhat of a loss in determining what music might be suitable for a particular dance combination. This situation tends to arise more frequently in center work than with the combinations given at the barre. In such situations, the accompanist should not feel reluctant or embarrassed to ask the instructor for more explanation or information and perhaps for the opportunity to try out several different musical selections. It is true that the skillful accompanist will rarely need to interrupt the flow of the class for this purpose, and as time is very valuable to the dance instructor, it should be avoided as much as possible. However, the dance instructor should be particularly understanding and patient in the case of inexperienced accompanists. Asking an occasional question is preferable to fouling up a dance combination, and a question here and there from the pianist may help to avert a situation in which the dance instructor must interrupt the combination because the music is unsuitable. This wastes much valuable class time.

Uniform Musical Phrases

Any dance combination given by an instructor in a classical ballet class will be, almost without exception, structured to accommodate musical phrases which are square and even. This does not necessarily hold true in a class of modern dance, but it is not within the scope of this text to discuss the techniques of accompanying modern dance. In a ballet class, however, the sequence of dance steps will fall into four, eight, sixteen, and thirty-two bar phrases. Even if the instructor gives a dance combination which has an unusual meter such as ⅝ or ⅞ (which is extremely rare), the phrases will most likely be square and even. Bearing the above facts in mind, the ballet pianist should prepare himself and his music in such a way as to make certain that he always cadences in the proper measure of music, ends combinations with the dancers, and plays in even musical phrases. This is not to say that the pianist should not investigate music which is unsquare in its phrase structure (for example, music in phrases of seven or perhaps eleven bars), because in many cases he can easily perform some kind of musical surgery which will make the music suitable for accompanying purposes (making it into phrases of eight bars), while leaving the musical sense of the piece intact, logical, and acceptable.

Various methods will be discussed later for arranging music with uneven phrases so that it may be suitable for ballet accompaniment. Meanwhile, it should be forcefully stated that the pianist who turns his back on a nice piece of music in considering it for use in the ballet class, solely because the music is not square or not immediately usable, is depriving himself. He may perhaps lift only a phrase or two, or he may take a particular harmonic progression which he can expand on his own into an entirely independent musical idea. This kind of imagination, flexibility, and creativity is essential for anyone who wants to accompany for the ballet and do it well.

It is not at all uncommon that an entire dance combination will consist, for example, of three sixteen-measure phrases, rather than four sixteen-measure phrases. In other words, the combination may end at forty-eight measures rather than sixty-four, or at twenty-four measures rather than thirty-two. This is by no means always clear to the accompanist ahead of time. Indeed, it is not always apparent to the instructor, until the end of the combination. If the pianist is on the alert, there will be no serious difficulty. Since the accompanist knows that the musical phrase will be a square one, he need not worry from measure to measure about exactly when the combination will end. He will quickly learn whether or not it is time to cadence at the end of a particular phrase, by watching the dancers or by receiving an indication from the instructor. The end of any dance combination should be finished naturally and gracefully, in a musical fashion. It should not be abruptly or unexpectedly chopped off so that the dancers are left hanging in the air.

Preparations and Their Functions

Different ballet instructors always have their own personal idiosyncrasies and methods of teaching class. There are, however, certain procedures which are observed in the ballet studio which are so universal and basic that it is essential to discuss them, since they directly involve the accompanist. One such procedure is the practice of having the accompanist give a musical preparation for each dance combination. At the outset of any dance combination, there is generally a brief musical introduction (or preparation), which may vary in its length and other features. It may be simply two chords (a dominant and a tonic, for example), or perhaps an arpeggio. It may be a two-bar or four-bar phrase, or eight beats of a left-hand ostinato. The method of giving the preparation will be illustrated in detail in Chapter 4. Let it suffice here to say that the accompanist is generally expected to give a preparation, and experience will cue him as to the most suitable kind of preparation to play. The purpose of the preparation is to enable the dancers to prepare and position themselves properly for the combination. The preparation also indicates to the dancers what the tempo of the combination will be. If the accompanist plays the preparation at one tempo and then proceeds to play the combination at a different tempo, confusion will abound. He must therefore make certain to give the preparation in a tempo which is uniform with that of the combination to follow.

Ending Combinations with the Dancers

The ability of the dance accompanist to consistently end his music to coincide with the end of a combination requires constant alertness and is a skill which takes some time to perfect. When a dance instructor demonstrates or explains a dance combination to the class he may do it rather hastily, at least as far as the accompanist is concerned. The dancers will understand what the instructor has in mind, whereas many times the accompanist will find himself in considerable doubt as to how much music a given combination will require. The accompanist need not, however, feel totally confused. He may assume with considerable assurance that the combination will be designed to fit even, square phrases of music. His challenge is not to end too soon or too late. If the accompanist remains poised and is ready to cadence at the end of each major phrase, while keeping one eye on the teacher, he will generally, with a little practice, be able to end at the proper time.

Occasionally the accompanist will find that he has ended a combination, only to observe that the class is still dancing. He has probably become too absorbed in his own playing to notice one of several possible reasons for this. Either he himself has failed to calculate the amount of music required and has stopped too soon, or perhaps the instructor has decided unexpectedly to have the combination repeated and has so indicated without much warning to the accompanist. One effective technique for compensating for this situation (especially with faster combinations) is to continue counting beats after the combination has apparently ended. In this way, the accompanist knows exactly where he is, in terms of the beats in a measure, and with a little practice can jump back into the music quite readily. He has no time to grope around for the right beat in such a spot, but has to react very speedily in order not to confound the dancers and disrupt the combination. The accompanist can be even more on top of the situation by not only counting after he thinks the combination is over, but by continuing to play silently on the surface of the keyboard. This method is nearly infallible and will bail the accompanist out of the situation outlined above every time. He has only to depress the keys again and he is exactly where he should be in the music.

After the dancers have come away from the barre and are working out on the dance floor during the second phase of the class, the accompanist's responsibility to end with them occasions the same problems. Especially toward the end of the ballet class, the dancers are involved with steps and combinations in which they start at one corner of the studio and dance diagonally to the opposite corner, or they may simply dance from one side of the studio to the other. They may do this singly, in pairs, four at a time, or in larger groups. In such cases, the pianist, after having given an appropriate introduction (preparation) for the first group of dancers, will then merely continue to play for some indefinite period of time while each succeeding group of dancers prepares and begins at each four, eight, or sixteen measures of music (whatever the instructor wishes). Occasionally the instructor may ask the accompanist to insert a preparation into the music every sixteen bars, for example, to prepare the next group of dancers. In this case the music does not stop between groups of dancers, but two or four introductory measures will be inserted at regular appropriate intervals. Various aspects of this kind of accompanying will later be discussed in more detail.

Changing Sides and Reversing Combinations

Two procedures basic to the ballet class are doing combinations on both sides and reversing combinations.

All combinations are danced on both sides, on the right and on the left (generally in that order). There are two main reasons why this is done. (1) It enables the dancers to derive more benefit from the combination by allowing them to do it twice, as in the case of pliés. (2) In many dance combinations, one leg is designated as the supporting leg, while the other is designated as the working leg. As in the case of frappés or ronds de jambes, for example, the leg upon which the major weight of the body is placed is designated as the supporting leg, while the other leg, which is left to maneuver freely, is designated as the working leg. Thus, changing sides with each combination reverses the supporting and working roles. In this way, both legs get balanced exercise, which is very important.

The accompanist should therefore expect to play for each combination twice and sometimes more than twice, if the instructor desires. The instructor may choreograph the combination in such a way that the changing from one side to the other is worked into the musical phrase. In this case, the accompanist will not need to stop the music between sides, but will play continuously. If he is alert and observant, he will realize that the dancers have changed sides, particularly while they are at the barre, because they will pivot and face the opposite direction. If the dancers are out on the floor, as in center work, they will simply dance in the opposite direction. Of course, in some combinations the dancers may change sides several times. In cases where the dancers pause between sides (which is most of the time) to orient themselves and to rest briefly, the accompanist must stop, and then at the appropriate time give the preparation again and begin the combination on the other side. In a continuous exercise during which the dancers change sides but do not pause, the preparation is, of course, omitted, unless the instructor specifically requests to have it.

The instructor may also ask the dancers to reverse the combination. In this case, the accompanist simply uses the same music which he used for the original combination. When a dance combination is reversed, the dancer's working leg moves in the direction opposite to the direction in which it moved in the original combination. In other words, if a dancer were doing a tendu exercise in which his working leg is extended in front of him, his working leg is then extended behind him when the dance combination is done in reverse. Reversing a combination does not mean that the original combination is literally done backwards.

As is the case when the dancers change sides in a combination, the instructor may or may not choose to have a pause between the original combination and the one done in reverse. It is of course possible for the dancers to execute a combination, reverse it, change sides, reverse it again, etc., without ever pausing. As always, it is the responsibility of the accompanist to remain alert. It becomes aggravating to a dance instructor when he has to work with an accompanist who never stops playing at the ends of combinations, but continues to play on after the dancers have finished (probably because he has his head buried in the music, and is not looking at the class).

Thinking Ahead

As the ballet accompanist becomes more experienced in playing for classes, he will be more and more able to anticipate in a general way, and with fair accuracy, what the next dance combination will be. This is particularly true with the order of combinations in the barre work, where the sequence is fairly well established. Different instructors vary in their approach to teaching classes, and as the accompanist becomes more familiar with the instructors as individuals, he will be in a better position to anticipate their routines. The reader may refer to the chapters of this book which deal specifically with the barre and center in a detailed manner. But let it be stated here that, particularly in cases in which the accompanist does not readily improvise, or does not have his scores memorized, it is a wise idea to think a combination or two ahead and to be prepared. As an example, if the class has just finished doing their plié combinations at the barre, the accompanist may assume with relative certainty that the following combination will be tendus. The tendus will probably be slow or possibly of a moderate tempo. After the tendus will probably come battements tendus dégagés. If these are omitted the next exercise will probably be either fondus or ronds de jambes. In thinking ahead in such a manner and in knowing what kind of music is suitable for each step, the accompanist will be able either to prepare himself mentally by deciding what to improvise or play from memory, or he will be locating the appropriate scores and placing them where they will be immediately available when he requires them.

Given the circumstances in which the ballet accompanist finds himself, it is a very practical idea for him to compile some organized notebooks of dance music. Suggestions of methods for accomplishing this are given in Chapter 3. It is also wise, whenever possible, to be prepared to play instantly any one of three or four different pieces for the same dance combination, as one piece or another may turn out not to be suitable for one reason or another. Being prepared in this way, the accompanist will save much class time and will avoid making the dancers and the instructor stand around while he is locating suitable music. The accompanist will thereby also avoid personal embarrassment and discomfort at having inconvenienced the members of the class.

Memorizing Music

At this point it is appropriate to admonish the ballet accompanist to prepare himself further for dance class by having as much of his repertory memorized as possible. Along with constantly striving to improve his skills of improvization, he should also gradually be committing more and more music to memory. As has been previously stated, the accompanist should have his music catalogued and well organized in some fashion. This becomes increasingly important as he compiles more and more music. Even when all of his music is carefully organized, however, he will find that there are times in dance class (for instance, when the instructor unexpectedly asks him to change to another piece, or when the accompanist himself discovers that the music which he is using simply does not work at the tempo desired) when it will be greatly to his advantage to be able to jump immediately to another selection without having to search for the score.

The accompanist will also frequently find himself in situations where he plays uninterruptedly for relatively long periods of time (perhaps as long as fifteen minutes), and a change of music is advisable (as in a medley of pieces). This is often the case with diagonal combinations in which the dancers proceed one after the other or in groups across the floor. Changing music during long, continuous combinations will help to conserve the strength of the accompanist and will avoid the dreary mental predicament in which he finds himself pounding out the same measures over and over again. The accompanist will of course not be able to change music if he has nothing memorized and cannot reach for a convenient score in the midst of a combination.

Practicing Repertory at Varying Tempos

The accompanist will be in an even more secure position mentally if he has practiced his music at many different tempos, trying while doing so to make them sound musically acceptable and natural. In accompanying for ballet classes, it is not at all uncommon that, halfway through a combination (particularly one at the barre), the accompanist will be asked by the instructor to increase the tempo, often significantly, and sometimes to double it. (For that matter, the instructor may adjust the tempo of a combination at any time if he feels that it is too fast or too slow.) If the pianist finds himself encumbered by a piece which has too many notes, he will be bogged down and get into trouble. This situation arises more frequently with some steps than with others (for example, it occurs more with tendus and frappés than with ronds de jambes, and it almost never occurs during pliés or adagios, at least not as dramatically) and is more characteristic of some instructors than others. Dance instructors will sometimes choreograph a combination with a preset tempo change and will occasionally desire a musical setting which changes abruptly in tempo and in style. The accompanist should be informed ahead of time in such cases. In light of the above discussion, it is not only advisable that the pianist practice his repertory at varying tempos, but that he practice changing tempos frequently and without pause within the context of any given piece of music.

Looking Up

The ballet accompanist must be able to keep his eyes on the dance class while playing. He should try to watch them as much as possible, and he will not be able to do this if his eyes are buried in a piece of music or riveted on his hands. Considering the previous discussion concerning memorization, one more significant reason can now be cited in support of knowing scores from memory. It enables the accompanist to look up and watch the dancers. This is a key principle in dance accompaniment, and it needs to be practiced. It is difficult for most pianists to get into the habit of watching, because they are so accustomed to concentrating entirely upon themselves. The pianist who has done ensemble work will have had some experience in devoting part of his attention to others while playing. But even in the case of chamber music, the accompanist's attention toward the other members of the ensemble is more auditory than visual. The dance accompanist must be sufficiently skilled that he can partly separate himself from his own music and motor activity (never completely, to the point of losing control) and divide his mental attention between himself and the dancers. When he accomplishes this, he will have taken a major step in mastering dance accompaniment, and he will be much more adept at avoiding the problems which confront the inexperienced accompanist, such as running on and on after the dancers have finished the combination. In time and with experience, the dance accompanist increasingly resembles a very sensitive barometer which reflects and supports what the dancers are doing on the dance floor. The mature dance accompanist accommodates the dancers almost instantly, and his playing reflects and enhances the quality of the dance movements. This is the heart of good ballet accompaniment, and it requires the accompanist's visual attention towards the dancers.

Accompanying at the Proper Dynamic Level

The ballet accompanist should make an effort to play for dance classes at a dynamic level which is in keeping with the situation. Since circumstances vary, the accompanist may need to make some corresponding adjustments in his playing. Much will depend on the quality, size, and style of the piano being used.

Music for ballet class should never dwindle in dynamic or rhythmic intensity to the point that it becomes vague or indistinct. If the accompaniment is so weak that the dancer cannot readily discern the phrase and pulse, the whole purpose of the music will be lost. Weak music interferes seriously with the mental processes of the dancer, because in straining to grasp the music, his concentration on himself, which is essential, is broken. This is not to say that the dancer should not be attentive to the music—he should always be aware of it. However, the music should support him, but not interfere with or distract him.

In general, the dynamic level of the accompaniment will not need to be as imposing during the barre exercises as it may be during the center work. An accompanist can make himself rather obnoxious if he is hammering away unnecessarily. This is particularly true of smooth, slow, graceful combinations like pliés and fondus. Boisterous music is out of context with such combinations. Let it be reiterated once more, at the risk of being overly repetitious, that the proper musical support must always be there. Extremes are to be avoided. The accompanist may make his playing as full and as rich as he wishes, almost to the point of gushing, without becoming overpowering.

During much of the center work, particularly in the case of certain grand allegro combinations, the dancers need all the support and thrust which the accompanist can supply. This is especially true with the big waltzes. In this situation, the accompanist will want to approximate as nearly as possible a full symphony orchestra. Such demands can be extremely taxing. Other combinations should be accompanied by very light, bouncy music, whereas at times a very solid, even heavy piece of music is most suitable. In general, however, no matter what the nature of the music or the combination is, a plodding, earthbound, stagnant character in the music should be avoided at all costs. This kind of accompanying brings the dancers down in the worst way and makes them feel as if they had weights tied to their ankles.

During some combinations, the instructor may need to communicate verbally with the dancers, for the purpose of counting out the beats, giving corrections, or calling out the next step. In many such cases, it would be a matter of courtesy for the accompanist to soften his playing by a dynamic level or two to save the instructor's voice. This advice to the accompanist is, like the advice concerning dynamic levels in general, more applicable with some dance combinations than with others. It applies particularly to the slower barre exercises, including stretches, pliés, fondus, etc. In the case of grand allegro steps in general, and particularly in the case of big waltzes, such accommodations should not be made. It gives the effect of dropping the floor out from under the dancers.

In light of the above discussion, the accompanist (taking into consideration the nature of the piano on which he is playing) may want to open the lid of the piano. For center work in general it is frequently a good idea. The accompanist does not have to work as hard. It would of course be absurd for the accompanist to jump up and down with every combination to open or close the lid. However, the general circumstances may warrant having the lid open. (Bear in mind that it is usually feasible to open the tops of upright pianos, as well as the lids of grands.) The size and acoustics of the dance studio are another factor to consider.

Barre and Center Combinations

The ballet class is divided into barre and center work, each comprising about half of the class time (although the amount of time devoted to each will vary with the individual instructor and the level of advancement of the dance students). The barre work consists of a series of exercises which prepares and trains the dancer for the dance steps which are dealt with in the center. As the accompanist studies the lists and discussions of the barre and center steps which follow, he should bear in mind that the order in which the exercises and steps are discussed reflects a general order and format which is usually followed in the ballet class, but which is relatively flexible, particularly where the center work is concerned.

Besides training the dancer for the steps which are used in the center, the work at the barre serves to warm up the dancer's muscles gradually and systematically, while toning and training them. The feet, ankles, calves, thighs, hips, stomach, back, arms, and neck all receive attention. Proper work in the center is not possible unless the dancer works properly at the barre. Any faults or flaws in the barre work will be exposed and magnified in the center. Thus, barre work provides a foundation which must be absolutely correct and solid. The barre offers additional support and balance to the dance student and facilitates the learning of steps. In beginning ballet classes, the majority of class time will probably be taken for barre work.

The list of barre exercises does not include by any means all of the exercises which could be done at the barre. It does include the major ones, however. The order of the barre exercises is fairly routine, at least for the major steps. Stretches may or may not be done. If they are not done, pliés always begin the class. A separate port de bras may be done, or it may be included with the pliés. More than one plié combination may be given. The instructor will probably give at least two tendu combinations which are usually followed by ronds de jambe or perhaps by fondus. The steps which then follow may vary—perhaps frappés, développés, or other combinations. The last exercises at the barre will probably be grands battements of one kind or another. At the end of the barre work, the dancers may do a series of stretches together, or they may limber up individually before beginning the center work. The descriptions of the different exercises at the barre and in the center which follow are accompanied by appropriate general suggestions for musical accompaniment. In Chapter 3, the subject of suitable repertory for specific steps and combinations will be dealt with extensively.

In studying the diagram of the center steps and the discussions of the individual steps which follow, the accompanist should bear in mind the following. The list of dance steps is subdivided into different categories according to the type of step: adagios, linking steps, petit allegro steps, pirouettes, and grand allegro steps. The list is not exhaustive, but it does include most of the major dance steps. It should be clearly understood that many of the steps in the various respective categories are not by any means performed exclusively by themselves or only with other steps in the same category. The essence of choreography is the combination of many different kinds of dance steps. Therefore, one will find, for instance, petit allegro steps in grand allegro combinations, and vice versa. There are of course some steps which may not work well together in a particular combination.

In the context of this book, for the purpose of simplifying matters somewhat from the point of view of the accompanist, the steps are discussed as if they were being done individually, by themselves (not in conjunction with other steps). In this way the accompanist can get a capsule idea of each step, along with some indication as to what kind of tempo and meter will be suitable for it. The steps may be choreographed into many workable combinations. From studying the text, the accompanist can develop for himself a concept about what kind of music is required for combinations which involve various predominant

for the first combination; a moderate to quick ²⁄₄ or ⁴⁄₄ for the second combination.

BATTEMENT TENDU JETÉ (BATTEMENT TENDU DÉGAGÉ). Jeté means thrown. This exercise is very similar to battements tendus, except that in this exercise, the toes are allowed to come slightly off the floor. The foot is "thrown" away from the standing position.

Music: The music for battements tendus dégagés is generally moderate to quick in tempo. The rhythm should be sharp and clear, and well accented: a sharp ²⁄₄, ⁴⁄₄, or ⁶⁄₈.

POINTÉ. Meaning pointed, and designating the position in which the leg is stretched away from the starting position. Only the toes are touching the floor, and are lifted from the floor in quick, light movements. The toe taps the floor lightly. This teaches the muscles of the leg to move quickly.

Music: Since pointés are generally a rather fast exercise, the music should be correspondingly fast and light: a quick ²⁄₄, ⁴⁄₄, or ⁶⁄₈.

FONDU. A melting or sinking down. A plié on one leg, causing the body to be lowered. In its general character and grace, this movement is much like pliés, but perhaps a little quicker.

Music: The music for fondus is similar to that used for pliés, although it may be a little bit brighter: a slow to moderate ³⁄₄ or ⁴⁄₄.

ROND DE JAMBE À TERRE. A circle of the leg on the ground. The working leg traces a circular movement on the floor. The toe of the working leg stays in contact with the ground, and both legs are kept straight. This exercises loosens the hips and strengthens the ankles.

Music: This exercise calls for a smooth even waltz feeling, although the accompanist need not by any means always feel compelled to play a waltz. Many pieces in triple meter would be suitable, and the tempo may vary considerably: a smooth ³⁄₄ or rather broad ⁶⁄₈.

ROND DE JAMBE EN L'AIR. A circle of the leg in the air. The working leg is opened to second position in the air. The toe makes an oval in the air, the foot moving in towards the body and then away from it. The upper part of the working leg must remain still while the lower part of the leg moves. This teaches the dancer to isolate the parts of the working leg and to control the moving parts.

Music: The music for this combination may vary, because of the range of tempos. This ronds de jambe exercise will most likely be somewhat quicker than the preceding ronds de jambe exercise: possibly an energetic ¾, or a moderate ²/₄ or ⁴/₄.

BATTEMENT FRAPPÉ. Striking or struck battement. The heel of the working foot touches or "beats" the ankle of the supporting leg, and the ball of the working foot strikes the floor, finishing several inches off the floor. The upper leg remains immobile. Frappés strengthen the ankles and feet and teach the dancer to execute and control quick, sharp movements.

Music: The tempo for this combination will vary, although the music should be very marked and distinct, with a well-punctuated rhythm. A duple meter is usually the most suitable: a sharp ²/₄ or ⁴/₄.

BATTEMENT SUR LE COU-DE-PIED. Beating at the "neck" of the foot (ankle). The working foot is wrapped around the ankle of the supporting leg. The heel of the working foot rapidly beats in front and then in back of the supporting ankle. This exercise prepares the dancer for batterie, or jumps with beats.

Music: The music for this combination will generally be very fast and correspondingly light, even nervous: a very fast ²/₄, ⁴/₄, or ⁶/₈.

PAS DE CHEVAL. Horse's step. This exercise is reminiscent of the movement of the horse's hoof as it paws the ground with one leg. The chief purpose of pas de cheval is to increase the dexterity and flexibility of the dancer's foot.

Music: The most suitable music for this step is usually a moderate ²/₄ or ⁴/₄.

DÉVELOPPÉ. Developed. The working leg is drawn up along the supporting leg and is opened into the air. The hips remain straight and square. This exercise is done slowly and smoothly, without jerking · movements and without disturbing the rest of the body.

Music: The music for développés should be slow and graceful and will be very similar in style to the music used for pliés and fondus: a slow, smooth ¾ or ⁴/₄.

GRAND BATTEMENT. Large battement. The purpose of this exercise is to loosen the hip joints and to turn out the legs from the hips. The working leg is raised upward and away from the original position to maximum height and then brought back down again. The movement of the working leg should not throw the body or hips out of proper placement. The working leg may be raised in any of several directions.

Music: Grands battements require a strong, forceful music with a heavy downbeat. A march is excellent in most cases: a strong ²/₄ or ⁴/₄.

BATTEMENT EN CLOCHE. Battement like a bell. A type of grand battement in which the working leg swings freely from front to back, resembling the pendulum of a clock. The body is kept still. This exercise loosens the hips, but should not interfere with the general placement of the body.

Music: Music for battements en cloche should be in a strong, swinging triple meter, with a heavy downbeat: a swinging ³/₄ or ⁶/₈.

STRETCHES (OPTIONAL). Before coming into the center after the barre work is finished, the dancers may do a series of stretches, either individually or together. Music may or may not be required.

Music: The kind of music required, if any, will depend on the nature of the stretches, but it will most likely be comparable to the music used either for the beginning stretches or the pliés.

Center Dance Steps Chart

Adagio
Temps Lié

Linking Steps
Glissade
Pas de Bourée
Chassé

Petit Allegro
Assemblé
Ballonné
Ballotté
Brisé
Brisé Volé

Changement
Coupé
Echappé Changé Sauté
Emboîté
Entrechat
Jeté
Jeté Passé
Pas de Chat
Sauté
Saut de Basque
Sissone (Ouverte, Fermée)
Soubresaut
Temps Levé

Pirouettes
Slow, in Place
  Attitude
  Arabesque
  Other Posés
  From 4th ⎫
  From 5th ⎬ Preparation from Two Feet
  From 2nd ⎭
  En Promenade

Quick, in Place
  From 5th
  Flic-Flac (En Tournant)
  Fouetté

Quick, Moving
  Assemblé Soutenu en Tournant
  Chainné (Déboulé)
  Piqué Posé

Tour en l'Air (Men's Step)

Rising Steps
Relevé
Sous-Sus

Grand Allegro
Cabriole
Grand Échappé
Grand Jeté en Avant
Jeté en Tournant (par Terre)
Grand Jeté Entrelacé
Grand Jeté en Tournant
Pas Balancé
Pas de Basque (Grand)
Pas de Ciseaux
Pas de Poisson
Pas Failli
Renversé Sauté
Sauté Fouetté
Sissonne Tombée

(Fast pirouettes, in place and moving;
tour en l'air)

Révérence

*The Center: Discussion of Steps
and General Music Requirements*

Adagio

At ease, at leisure. An adagio is a combination made up of various movements. It is generally slow, graceful, and drawn out. It teaches control and stamina to the dancer. Its principal difficulty and challenge lies in the great demands it makes on the dancer's ability to execute beautiful, slow, continuous movements without showing strain, fatigue, or lack of control. Temps lié is a step which is frequently used in adagios. It teaches control in the transference of weight from one foot to the other.

Music: Depending on the nature of the adagio, the music will vary somewhat in its general mood and feeling. However, adagios are generally comprised of one or more of the following qualities: gracefulness, stateliness, continuity of movement, sustained poses, smoothness, elegance, and sweeping, expressive gestures. The music should be correspondingly slow, full, broad, etc.: a ¾ or ⁴⁄₄ of expressive quality.

Linking Steps

GLISSADE. PAS DE BOURRÉE. CHASSÉ. These three dance steps may be used in virtually any dance combination. They are linking steps, in that they are used to link other steps together. In other words, they get the dancer from one step to another. They may be practiced as separate, individual steps in beginning dance classes; in this case, the tempo and feeling of the music will vary, depending on the approach of the teacher. Appropriate music may be selected as the occasion demands. Since they are generally used in the context of other steps, they are mentioned here only for the accompanist's general information.

Petit Allegro

Note: The music for petit allegro will be discussed as a whole, after the petit allegro steps which follow are dealt with individually.

ASSEMBLÉ. Assembled, joined together. As the foot of the working leg is brushed out along the floor, the supporting leg pushes off the floor, into the air. The legs are joined together (assembled) in the air before the dancer returns to the ground.

BALLONNÉ. Bounced, like a ball. As the supporting leg pushes the dancer off the ground, the working leg does a battement. As the supporting leg returns to the floor, the working leg finishes so that the foot touches the ankle of the supporting leg.

BALLOTTÉ. Tossed. The body does a backward and forward swaying movement in the air, as the weight changes from one leg to the other. The legs open sharply in the air.

BRISÉ. Broken or beating. A brisé is like an assemblé with beats, which travels. It covers space.

BRISÉ VOLÉ. Flying brisé. This brisé is finished on one foot, the other leg crossed in front or in back, allowing the dancer to do another brisé in the opposite direction, finishing on the opposite foot.

CHANGEMENT. Changing. A jump which begins with both feet and finishes on both feet, but the feet change positions in the air, so that the one which was originally in front ends in back.

COUPÉ. Cut or cutting. A small jump or step from one foot to the other, used as a preparation for other steps. This term also designates the position of the working foot at the ankle of the supporting leg.

ÉCHAPPÉ CHANGÉ SAUTÉ. Escaping with a jump. This step involves two jumps in succession. It is begun from two feet, the legs opening before landing. The second jump which immediately follows brings the feet back together.

EMBOÎTÉ. Fitted together, or boxed. This is a small, travelling jump from one leg to the other, in which the working leg always finishes at coupé in front of the ankle of the supporting leg.

ENTRECHAT, EVEN-NUMBERED AND ODD-NUMBERED. Interweaving, braiding; a beating step. The dancer jumps off the floor and quickly crosses the legs before and behind each other. Entrechats are numbered from two through ten, depending on the number of crossings: deux, quatre, six, huit, dix, the dancer lands on two feet; trois, cinq, sept, neuf, he lands on one foot.

JETÉ. Thrown. Many kinds. This is a jump from one leg to the other. The working leg is "thrown" out as the supporting leg pushes off into the air.

JETÉ PASSÉ. A jeté passed forward (en avant) or backward (en arrière). In this step, the legs cross, resembling the action of a pair of scissors.

PAS DE CHAT. Cat's step. Pas de chat is a travelling jump, which resembles in its movement the leap of a cat. The legs are drawn up quickly, one after the other, while the dancer is in the air.

SAUTÉ. Jumped or jumping. A sauté is a simple jump. It can be done in many positions and may stay in place or travel.

SAUT DE BASQUE. A Basque jump. The dancer turns in the air, with one foot drawn up to the knee of the other leg. The landing is on one foot. One or two turns may be executed during the jump. In the latter case, the jump is designated as double saut de basque.

SISSONNE (OUVERTE OR FERMÉE). A travelling jump, named after the originator. In sissonne ouverte, the dancer jumps off two legs and finishes on one leg. In sissonne fermée, the dancer begins and finishes the jump on two legs. Both sissonnes travel in the air.

SOUBRESAUT. A sudden spring. This jump begins from both feet. As the feet push off the floor, they are held tightly together, well pointed. The knees are straight. It may travel in any direction.

TEMPS LEVÉ. A raising motion. Temps levé is a hop which is done from one foot and lands on that same foot. It can be done in any position.

Music for petit allegro steps: In discussing suitable music for the above petit allegro steps, it will be appropriate to treat them as a whole. These steps may be worked on individually or in many different combinations. However, any one step or combination of steps in this category will fall into a common range of musical tempos and feelings: namely, moderate to bright $2/4$ and $4/4$ meters. Occasionally, a bright, dancy $3/4$ may be required to give a little extra time or lift for the steps. Regardless of individual variations, the music required should be very lively and bright, light and dancy. The quality of the music should not pull the dancers down or make them feel sluggish. Rather, the music should help the dancers to get up into the air. It should convey a sense of buoyancy, or bounce. A light polka or one of the livelier Chopin waltzes is often ideal. If the accompanist chooses a waltz for a petit allegro combination and the tempo seems too rushed or stiff, it is a good indication that a $2/4$ meter should be substituted. On the other hand, if the accompanist decides to play a $2/4$ or $4/4$ meter and the music is hopelessly sluggish, then a bright $3/4$ will probably work much better. Given the circumstances, one meter will tend to fill out the space a little better than the other. Everything depends on the individual dance combination.

Pirouettes

Pirouettes are turns. They can be done on one or two feet, in place or travelling. It will be convenient from the point of view of the accompanist to divide pirouettes into three basic, arbitrary categories: (1) pirouettes done slowly, in place; (2) pirouettes done quickly, in place; and (3) pirouettes done quickly, while travelling. Many pirouettes are practiced at the barre, but it will be most practical here to discuss them in relation to center work. Any discussion about appropriate music may be applied to pirouettes at the barre when the need arises.

Slow, in place

ATTITUDE, ARABESQUE, AND OTHER POSÉS. These pirouettes are done on one spot, on one foot, in a slow and controlled manner. They are frequently used in adagio combinations in conjunction with other steps.

Music: In general, these movements will warrant music with an adagio-like quality, smooth and sustained. Particularly in the case of attitudes, a slow to moderate waltz tempo may be appropriate.

PREPARATION FROM TWO FEET. Turns from fourth, fifth, and second position are done on one foot, but prepared from two feet. They are done in place at a moderate tempo, and each pirouette may be comprised of one, two, three, or more turns, depending on the choreography or the ability of the dancers. They may be practiced alone or done in conjunction with other steps.

Music: Music for the above turns will be of a moderate tempo and of a relatively smooth quality in most cases. A moderate waltz, rather rich and full, may work well in many instances. Occasionally, a very broad 4/4 meter will work more successfully than a 3/4. The choice between a 3/4 or 4/4 will depend on various factors analogous to those discussed in the section on petit allegro.

EN PROMENADE. In a walk. This is a very slow turn, done on one flat foot. The supporting leg executes a series of small movements, whereby the supporting heel changes position by slight shifts. The rest of the body is in a posé. It is done in context with movements which have an adagio quality.

Music: The music used for any combination which employs promenades and comparable movements will have adagio qualities. The pianist should refer to the preceding discussion on adagio.

Quick, in place

FROM FIFTH POSITION. These pirouettes are done in place, rapidly, in succession. They are prepared from two feet and done on one foot.

Music: Music for this step should be bright and fast, a ²/₄ or ⁴/₄ only. A polka would be suitable. A cancan is ideal.

FLIC-FLAC (EN TOURNANT). A flicking movement, used in adagio, turning. The working foot executes the flicking movement in front of or behind the supporting leg as the body does a full turn. Flic-flac may be practiced at the barre, because of its difficulty.

Music: The music for flic-flacs should be a ²/₄ or ⁴/₄, similar in quality to the music for pirouettes from fifth position. However, the tempo will be somewhat more moderate.

FOUETTÉ. Whipped. Here, the dancer executes a full turn on one leg as the other leg whips the body around. These fast turns are done in place, in succession, on one foot.

Music: The music should be in the same style as that used for pirouettes from fifth position. Dancers may do sixteen in succession, even thirty-two or sixty-four, depending on the abilities of the dancers.

Quick, moving

ASSEMBLÉ SOUTENU EN TOURNANT, CHAINNÉ (DÉBOULÉ), PIQUÉ POSÉ. The above turns are all fast. Any number may be done rapidly in succession. In class, they may be done straight across the floor or in a diagonal from corner to corner. A number of dancers may form a large circle and perform them in that manner.

Music: The music for these steps will again be similar to that used for quick pirouettes in place: bright, fast ²/₄'s or ⁴/₄'s. The tempo may be extremely fast, in which case the accompanist will have to play very lightly and with all possible speed.

TOUR EN L'AIR. A turn in the air. This is almost exclusively a male dancer's step. It is done in place. The dancer leaps into the air, turning once, twice, perhaps several times (called single tour, double tour, etc.). These may be practiced in one spot, in succession, and are frequently used in many grand allegro combinations.

Music: The music for successive tours in place will either be a very large and powerful ¾ waltz tempo with a strong downbeat, or sometimes an equally assertive and powerful, broad ⁴/₄.

Rising Steps

RELEVÉ. SOUS-SUS. Raised, and under-over, respectively. Both relevés and sous-sus are rising steps—in performing these steps the dancer goes up quickly onto toe or half-toe. These steps are basic to dancing and are employed everywhere. They can be practiced at the barre or in the center and are often practiced by themselves in pointe class. Relevés can be done on one or two feet, and sous-sus is done on two feet, with one foot in front of the other, the legs and feet drawn tightly together, the heels forward.

Music: Music which is suitable for relevés and sous-sus, whether done at the barre or in the center, may be in a ²/₄ or ⁴/₄ meter and moderate in tempo. The character of the music should be sharp, clear, and well accented, although not too fast. These exercises may put considerable strain on the legs of the dancer, and a tempo which pushes too much will not be good for the dancer's muscles.

Grand Allegro

These steps usually come toward the end of the center work, when the dancers are really warmed up. They are bigger than petit allegro steps, generally big jumps which cover considerable space. They may be combined with various fast pirouettes and petit allegro steps. Here, the accompanist will need his biggest, most powerful waltzes, and fast, brilliant gallops, codas, and polkas.

CABRIOLE. A caper. The legs beat against each other while they are extended in the air during this big jump. The dancer lands on one leg.

Music: The most suitable music for this step is a big, powerful waltz, as is the case with many of the grand allegro steps.

GRAND ÉCHAPPÉ. A large escaping or slipping movement. This is a very big jump, usually done in place. It is a larger version of the échappé, which is also straight up and down.

Music: A ⁴/₄ is generally more suitable for grand échappé than a waltz is: a large, powerful ⁴/₄ or ²/₄, with a strong lift.

GRAND JETÉ EN AVANT. A large jeté forward. In this big forward leap, one leg pushes off the floor and is thrown up and back, while the other leg is thrown forward, into the air. While in the air, the dancer's legs form a splits, and he holds this position as long as possible. As he descends, he lands on the forward leg.

Music: Grand jeté en avant may be done in a typical big waltz combination. However, when the dancers are leaping across the floor in a straight line or in a circle, a strong $2/4$ or $4/4$ galop or coda is very good.

JETÉ EN TOURNANT (PAR TERRE). A jeté, turning across the floor. This is a large leap travelling forward, while staying close to the floor, followed by a complete turn in the air which lands on one foot.

Music: A fast, strong $2/4$ or $4/4$ meter is best for this step, which may be done in a straight line or in a circle: a galop or coda.

GRAND JETÉ ENTRELACÉ. Lacé refers to the "interlacing" of the legs. This is a large jump in which one foot is thrust forward, the body does a half turn to face the direction from which the jump originated, and the other leg is thrust towards the back, thus creating the interlacing effect.

Music: This step is usually done to a big waltz, like cabrioles or grand jeté en tournant.

GRAND JETÉ EN TOURNANT. A large jeté, turning. In this large jump, the dancer springs from one foot, throwing the other leg upward and around to the outside, while turning in the air.

Music: The most suitable music for this step is again a big, powerful waltz.

PAS BALANCÉ (BALANCÉ). A rocking step. This is a smooth, graceful, sweeping waltz step. It contains three steps in which the weight of the body is shifted from one foot to the other.

Music: A gracious, smooth, but dancy waltz is good for balancés. This step is not as big as many other grand allegro steps, and the music need not be so imposing.

PAS DE BASQUE (GRAND). A large Basque step. This step has three basic movements and is somewhat slower than most grand allegro steps. Both legs make large sweeping movements in the air.

Music: Pas de basque is best danced to a very slow, stately mazurka, or perhaps to a polonaise. A waltz is too fast and does not put enough emphasis on the individual beats within the measure.

PAS DE CISEAUX. Scissors step. One leg is thrown forward into the air as the dancer jumps off the ground. It then swings back past the other leg (thereby resembling scissors) as the dancer lands.

Music: The accompanist should use a large, strong waltz for pas de ciseaux.

PAS DE POISSON. Fish's step. The dancer jumps into the air, forming an arch with his back (resembling a fish leaping out of water). The legs are held straight and close together. The crossed feet resemble the tail of a fish.

Music: This step best fits into a ²/₄ or ⁴/₄ galop or coda tempo.

PAS FAILLI. Giving way. This step is similar to sissonne. The body does a slight turn in the air, so that the head begins to look over one shoulder. As the dancer lands, the back leg immediately slides forward, and the head finishes looking over the opposite shoulder.

Music: A strong ³/₄ or ⁴/₄ would be suitable for this step, depending on the tempo desired. The quality of the music will be comparable to that which is used for other grand allegro steps.

RENVERSÉ SAUTÉ. A jump, upset or reversed. The body bends so that the balance is angled, but controlled. The supporting leg pushes off from the floor in a jump, as the other leg does a battement front and circles to the back.

Music: Use the standard, strong grand allegro waltz for this step.

SAUTÉ FOUETTÉ. A sauté whipped. As the working leg does a battement from back to front, the supporting leg does a jump. When the working leg is lifted high to the front, the body does half a turn away from it, and the dancer finishes facing the opposite direction, with the working leg to the back.

Music: Usually the standard, strong grand allegro waltz is used. A strong ⁴/₄ with a lift may also work.

SISSONNE TOMBÉE. A sissonne falling. The dancer jumps off two feet and lands on one foot, immediately falling forward onto the other leg. This step is usually not practiced by itself, but is done with various other steps.

Music: Use the standard, strong grand allegro waltz.

Révérence

A curtsey. Many ballet classes end with a révérence, which basically is an elaborate series of bows. It may be combined with other elements. Its main purpose is to practice bowing. In bowing, the dancers generally acknowledge the instructor, the accompanist, and the real or imaginary audience.

Music: The music for the révérence will probably have a slow, adagio-like quality. It may be strong, assertive, and triumphant: a slow, or moderate ¾ or ⁴⁄₄ with a full, rich texture. Occasionally, a piece with a subdued, poetic quality lends a striking mood for révérence.

Suggested Piano
Repertory for Barre and
Center Work

Guidelines on Repertory

The following chapter is devoted to discussing suitable and representative piano literature which may be used in accompanying for ballet classes. It is divided into two major sections, the first dealing with barre exercises, the second with center steps. Each barre exercise and center step is treated individually or in conjunction with other combinations which warrant similar musical accompaniment. For each dance step there is a list of compatible compositions which musically reinforce the quality of the step. A wide variety of composers and styles has been suggested for most steps. This will enable the accompanist to acquire a broad, general musical feeling for each step, while learning about specific pieces which are individually suited for the purpose.

Several items of helpful information are included with each listing. For the accompanist's reference, the time signature of the piece is given, followed by a metronome marking which is intended to be a general indication of the appropriate tempo for each step when performed with that particular composition. The accompanist is reminded that this metronome suggestion indicates an average, comfortable tempo which may vary considerably in practical situations, depending on the taste of the instructor and his approach to teaching and on the abilities of the dancers. Following the metronome markings, the accompanist will find detailed, specific instructions concerning which measures of the music to use, where to cadence, and how to arrange measures into square and even musical phrases which will accommodate the dance combination. The accompanist will rarely use all of any given piece of music, and sometimes he will use only a small section, perhaps sixteen measures. He may take a handful of measures from different sections of the piece and knit them together into a continuous musical fabric.

The accompanist should be cautioned strongly against becoming too repetitious in using very short pieces or very short sections of larger pieces. For example, if the accompanist is using only sixteen measures of music to accompany a very long combination (particularly a fast-moving combination in which the music is used up rapidly) and has to repeat those measures over and over to fill out the exercise, the effect on the listener is deadening, to say the least. The accompanist should try to remedy this situation in one of two ways. If he has any skill at improvisation he can embellish, enrich, and decorate the music each time he repeats it. He should force himself to do this until he becomes relatively comfortable and proficient in doing so. The second alternative is simply to make sure that he has enough music available to avoid playing one phrase into the ground. By listening to the instructor demonstrate the combination, he should be able to ascertain at least roughly how much music he will need. Chapter 4 discusses in great detail many aspects of arranging and embellishing repertory and will suggest many ideas to the accompanist along these lines.

The accompanist should compare and coordinate the information in this chapter with that in the preceding chapter. He will thereby acquire an overall knowledge of the general structure of ballet classes, the approximate order and basic nature of the dance steps and their relationships to other steps, and a clear idea concerning which music is compatible with any particular dance step or combination of steps. The accompanist is encouraged to examine and analyze carefully the list of repertory suggestions, researching and employing whatever music he wishes, while drawing from his own repertory. The spectrum of music which is set forth in this chapter encompasses a wide range of styles and technical accessibility. Some of the music can be played readily, while other pieces will require considerable practice and preparation. Choice of repertory is left to the individual taste and ability of each accompanist. Many technically difficult pieces can be readily simplified for accompanying purposes, while retaining the essential features which make them good music for ballet. The accompanist is strongly encouraged to build up his own individual ballet repertory, rather than simply to go out and purchase ready-made collections of ballet pieces. This is very limiting, and does nothing to develop the latent talents of the accompanist. His musicality and powers of analysis will be much more stimulated to growth and development if he does most of his own research. Therefore, while the repertory lists provided in this chapter are fairly extensive and may be used as a syllabus, the primary purpose of this book is to provide adequate guidelines for individual research and selection of ballet repertory, by setting forth tried and reliable examples of usable music.

It is appropriate here to suggest one specific source of repertory which is not mentioned as a whole in the repertory lists which follow. This is the complete dances of Schubert (Franz Schubert, *Sämtliche Tänze,* 2 vols. München-Duisburg: G. Henle Verlag). Although this is a musical source which should not be overworked to the point of dreariness and boredom, it is mentioned here because it provides hundreds of small pieces in both duple and triple meter which are phrased clearly and evenly and which, for the most part, are readily playable. Included are minuets, waltzes, ländlers, ecossaises, and galops. The beginning accompanist can fall back on this readily available source of music while filling out his repertory with other composers and styles.

Another excellent source of potential music for class is Broadway music. Many of these show tunes are excellent for all kinds of steps, including bright, dancy waltzes, energetic $2/4$'s, lovely adagios, etc. This music lends a very nice change of pace from the straight classics.

Notebooks

It is a wise idea for the ballet accompanist to arrange and compile for himself notebooks of repertory for ballet class. This is practical for several reasons. Individual pieces are much easier to locate quickly when they are organized into notebooks. Notebooks may be arranged according to categories of dance steps or by composers. The best method is by composer, alphabetically. If the notebooks are arranged according to categories of dance steps, the question often arises as to the category under which a given piece of music should be classified. A piece of music is often suitable for many different steps. The more skilled the accompanist becomes at arranging and manipulating his repertory, the more possibilities any given piece of music will have for him. Therefore, arrangement of ballet notebooks by composer is the most practical method.

Assembling music into collections also avoids much unnecessary wear and tear on the accompanist's personal scores. He may have to carry his music around day after day, and he will often wish to write in alterations, measure numbers, notes, etc. This will soon deface and wear out his personal scores. Furthermore, he may use only one or two pieces out of an entire collection. There is little point to carrying around stacks of music volumes for only a few pieces. This is a real encumbrance for the accompanist and interferes with his ability to accompany efficiently. The longer an accompanist plays for ballet, the more repertory he will accumulate. Notebooks are an excellent solution to the problem of growing stacks of scores.

The accompanist is again encouraged to use as wide a variety of music as possible. This will help avoid becoming bored with the same repertory—a problem for the accompanist, the instructor, and the dancers. Besides researching the standard composers, the accompanist should always be open to any potential source of music, which may come from obscure sources.It is a good idea just to go to a music library if there is one available and begin thumbing through scores.

Avoidance of Standard Ballet Repertory

Among the repertory suggestions in this chapter, there are relatively few examples from the standard ballets. In general, it is a good idea to avoid as much of the standard ballet music as possible. If the dancers are professionals they will probably be nauseatingly familiar with the standard repertory. Hearing this music in class all the time and on the stage as well would be maddening. There are some times, however, when it is difficult for the accompanist to find good pieces which are as appropriate in feeling as ballet literature. For instance, traditional piano repertory offers little when it comes to finding appropriate (and technically accessible) music for fast pirouettes and $\frac{2}{4}$ grand allegro steps. In such instances, the codas, galops, and fast $\frac{2}{4}$'s from the ballet scores, as well as polkas, galops, and cancans, are ideal. In the section on music for grand allegro, appropriate suggestions are given.

Grand Allegro Waltzes

The accompanist is again reminded that many of the ²/₄ and ¾ combinations in grand allegro work may go on for a long time without pause, and in such circumstances his musical selections should not be so technically ambitious as to wear him out. To ease this strain, he might string together several different pieces, for esthetic and technical relief. If the accompanist has not committed a good deal of music to memory or does not improvise readily, he may wish to remove several compatible grand allegro pieces from his notebooks and line them up across the piano.

It is often difficult to find waltzes in the traditional piano repertory which convey ideally the sense of lift and energy which the dancers need in grand allegro waltzes. Most waltzes in the traditional piano repertory are, as written, too stylized—they do not possess that simple, ungarnished, elemental power which drives the dancers up into the air and inspires them to become unbound from the forces of gravity. Here, some of the big waltz melodies from Broadway do nicely.

With grand allegro waltzes in general, the first beat of each odd-numbered measure will be the beat on which the dancers push off from the ground. This beat should be correspondingly strong and powerful and should convey a sense of intense drive. Since the dancers will generally land on the first beat of the even-numbered measures, this beat should be comparatively lighter, so as not to encourage the sense of weight and heaviness. In other words, as a general principle in grand allegro waltzes, the heaviness of the downbeat of each successive measure will alternate as follows:

measure 1   heavy downbeat
measure 2   light downbeat
measure 3   heavy downbeat
measure 4   light downbeat   etc.

The grand allegro waltz should have a powerful bass. Octaves should be used on most left-hand downbeats rather than single notes. Furthermore, the most uplifting rhythmic motive should be employed in the right hand. One which conveys very well a sense of lift to the dancers may be illustrated as follows:

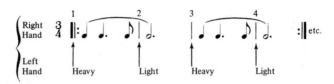

This motive would be put to excellent use in grand allegro waltzes, particularly in the odd-numbered measures during which the dancers push off from the ground.

Before concluding the discussion of grand allegro waltzes, it will be appropriate to make a point about playing accents in 2/4 combinations. Generally, the principle outlined above concerning a heavier downbeat on odd measures and a lighter downbeat on even measures will hold true here. This alternation of light and heavy beats gives the music life and prevents it from sounding stodgy and earthbound. For' example, this accenting would highlight very well a grand battement combination, during which the dancer's leg swings up briskly on the downbeat of the first measure and comes down lightly on the downbeat of the second measure. Naturally there are some instances when this principle does not apply: in a barre combination which employed consistently and conspicuously either very light or very heavy movements, the accompanist would want to highlight the dancer's movements accordingly.

In concluding the discussion on rhythmic accents, it should be pointed out in relation to the grand allegro waltzes and the characteristic motive illustrated above, that many waltzes may be arranged in such a way that their melodies duplicate this motive. The principles outlined above may be applied to almost any standard waltz. It merely requires that the melodies be somewhat rearranged or rewritten. Thus, an unlikely ¾ may be converted into a striking grand allegro waltz style. Of foremost importance is the manner in which the waltz is played, not what is written on the score. In fact, in the hands of a skilled accompanist, the same ¾ piece could be arranged in a number of ways, so as to be suitable for many combinations—pliés, ronds de jambes, a powerful grand allegro, etc. This is in fact nothing more than the principle of variation. Except for some outstanding thematic similarity, the dancers might not ever suspect that the same material was being used over and over again for different combinations. The methods for making such arrangements are the subject of Chapter 4.

Grasping the essence of feeling in grand allegro combinations (both ¾ and ⁴/₄) will probably be one of the most challenging problems for the inexperienced ballet accompanist. Whatever combination the accompanist is playing for, he should always attempt to convey and express the essential quality of the dance movements, whether they reflect the smoothness and grace of an adagio, or the sharp, accented brilliance of a petit allegro jumping step.

Need for Practical Experience

Practical experience is indispensable in learning the art of ballet accompaniment, and at some point the pianist must wade in and start to swim, so to speak, even if clumsily at first. The novice accompanist should observe different dance classes, noting the styles and skills of other more experienced and skilled accompanists. This is an excellent way to learn—by example. He should attend ballets, so that he may see the fruits and culmination of all the hard work done in the dance class. By doing these things, and by listening to ballets and to dance music, he will saturate his mind with the qualities that are essential to music for the dance.

The Barre

Music for pliés, port de bras (suitable for stretches)

Bach: Sarabande, English Suite in F Major
¾, MM quarter note equals 80
    Repeat the first eight measures, and play the remaining sixteen measures. This totals thirty-two measures. Repeat as necessary.

Bach: Menuet II, Partita in B-Flat Major
¾, MM quarter note equals 88
    Play entire movement straight through, taking repeats. This totals thirty-two measures. Repeat as necessary.

Brahms: Intermezzo, Op. 119 No. 2.
¾, MM quarter note equals 88
    Begin with the middle section, marked Andantino grazioso. Play the first thirty-two measures as written, and repeat as necessary.

Brahms: Romance in F Major
6/4, MM quarter note equals 80

Use the first sixteen measures. Since this piece is a 6/4, sixteen measures will be equivalent to thirty-two measures of 3/4. Repeat as necessary. In measure sixteen, cadence in F major, rather than in D minor.

Chopin: Nocturne in B Major, Op. 32 No. 1
4/4, MM quarter note equals 66

Use the first sixteen measures. Repeat as necessary. Cadence in B major in measure sixteen.

Chopin: Nocturne in E Major, Op. 62 No. 2
4/4, MM quarter note equals 66

Use the first sixteen measures. Measures seventeen through twenty-four may be repeated to form another sixteen-measure phrase. Cadence in B major in measure twenty-four after the repeat. This totals thirty-two measures. Repeat as needed.

Fauré: Nocturne in E-Flat Major, Op. 36
4/4, MM quarter note equals 50

Play the first eight measures. Omit measures nine through eleven, and play measures twelve through nineteen, cadencing in B-flat in measure nineteen. This totals sixteen measures of 4/4. Repeat as necessary.

Gershwin: Prelude No. 2 in C-Sharp Minor
4/4, MM quarter note equals 88

Play measures five through twelve for the first phrase, including the pickup to measure five. Play measures thirteen through eighteen for a second phrase, repeating measures fifteen and sixteen before playing measures seventeen and eighteen. The accompanist now has an even sixteen-measure phrase.

Play measures nineteen through twenty-six to complete the third eight-measure phrase. For the final eight-measure phrase, play measures twenty-seven through thirty, repeating twenty-nine and thirty, rounding out the phrase with two measures of F-sharp major. This totals thirty-two measures. Although these alterations sound rather elaborate, the accompanist will find that he can make the music sound quite smooth and convincing.

Rachmaninoff: Prelude in G-Flat Major, Op. 23 No. 10
¾, MM quarter note equals 60

Play measures three through thirty-four, including the pickup to measure three. This will make an even thirty-two-measure phrase. Cadence in G-flat major in measure thirty-four. Repeat as necessary.

Ravel: Waltz No. 2 in G Minor, Valses Nobles et Sentimentales
¾, MM quarter note equals 88

This piece falls into four equal sections of sixteen measures each, so no alterations are necessary.

Satie: Three Gymnopedies, No. 1
¾, MM quarter note equals 84

Measures five through twelve comprise the first phrase; measures thirteen through twenty-one (omitting twenty), the second. Measures twenty-two through thirty (omitting twenty-six) comprise the third phrase. The last phrase is made up of measures thirty-two through thirty-nine (omit measure thirty-one). This totals thirty-two measures of four even phrases. Repeat as necessary.

Wright and Forest: "Stranger in Paradise" from *Kismet*
⁴/₄, MM quarter note equals 88

Consider where the words start as measure one. Play measures one through sixteen as written and repeat as necessary. Cadence in F major in measure sixteen.

Music for fondus, développés, battements tendus (slow)

Brahms: Intermezzo, Op. 117 No. 1
⁶/₈, MM eighth note equals 92

Play measures one through sixteen, and cadence in E-flat major in measure sixteen. Repeat as necessary.

Brahms: Variations on a Theme by Paganini, Op. 35, Book I, Var. XI
²/₄, MM eighth note equals 50

This piece may be played straight through as written. It has sixteen measures. Repeat as necessary.

Brahms: Variations on a Theme by Paganini, Op. 35, Book II, Var. IV

⅜, MM eighth note equals 96

This piece may be played straight through as written. It has sixteen measures. Repeat as necessary.

Brahms: Waltz in E Major, Op. 39 No. 2
¾, MM quarter note equals 96

Play this waltz through without any alterations, taking the repeat after the first eight measures. This will total thirty-two measures. Repeat as necessary.

Brahms: Waltz in D Minor, Op. 39 No. 9
¾, MM quarter note equals 108

Play measures one through eight twice, then the remainder of the waltz, taking the second ending. This will total thirty-two measures. Repeat as necessary.

Brahms: Waltz in C-Sharp Minor, Op. 39 No. 16
¾, MM quarter note equals 96

Play the entire waltz as written, taking the repeat. This totals thirty-two measures. Repeat as necessary.

Chopin: Nocturne in F Minor, Op. 55 No. 1
⁴⁄₄, MM quarter note equals 80

Play measures one through sixteen, cadencing in F minor in measure sixteen. Repeat as necessary.

Chopin: Nocturne in C Minor, Op. 48 No. 1
⁴⁄₄, MM quarter note equals 60

Play measures one through sixteen, repeating them if necessary. The last time through, cadence in measure sixteen in C minor.

Gluck: Ballet des Ombres Heureuses from *Orpheo et Euridice*
¾, MM quarter note equals 88

Play measures one through eight twice. Then play measures nine through sixteen and measures seventeen through twenty-eight, omitting twenty-one through twenty-four. This will yield four smooth phrases of eight measures each. Repeat as necessary.

Granados: Valses Poeticos, No. 3

¾, MM quarter note equals 104

Play measures one through eight as written. For the second eight measures, play measures one through four again and then skip to measures nine through twelve. Play measures thirteen through twenty for the third phrase. For the last eight measures, play thirteen through sixteen again and then twenty-one through twenty-four. This process totals thirty-two measures. Repeat as necessary. Notice that this waltz was originally in twelve-measure phrases, through measure twenty-four.

Rachmaninoff: Variations on a Theme of Corelli, Op. 42 Var. IV
¾, MM quarter note equals 88

Play this piece straight through. It is sixteen measures long. Repeat as necessary.

Ravel: Mouvement de Menuet (II) from Sonatine
⅜, MM quarter note equals 88

For the first phrase, play measures one through four twice. Then play measures five through twelve. The third phrase will be measures thirteen through twenty. Measures twenty-one and twenty-two are omitted. The last phrase may be formed in this way: play measures twenty-three through twenty-six, then repeat measures twenty-three and twenty-four and round out the phrase with one measure of improvised A-flat major tonality. Cadence in the final measure on D-flat major. This will total four phrases of eight measures each. With a little bit of thought, the accompanist can make the above procedure sound quite natural and convincing. Repeat as necessary.

Saint-Saëns: Menuet in F Major, Op. 90
¾, MM quarter note equals 96

Play measures one through eight. The second phrase will be measures nine through twelve, played twice. Measures thirteen through twenty-four are identical to measures one through twelve, so the entire process may be repeated for these measures, yielding a total of thirty-two measures of four even phrases.

Schubert: Impromptu in A-Flat Major, Op. 142 No. 2
¾, MM quarter note equals 96

Play measures one through twenty-four to complete the first three phrases of eight measures each. The last eight-measure phrase may be done this way: play measures twenty-five through thirty as written and add two measures of suitable A-flat major tonality in which to cadence. Repeat as necessary.

Schumann: "Erinnerung" (Remembrance) from Album for the Young, Op. 68
2/4, MM quarter note equals 52

Play measures one through ten, omitting measures seven and eight, for the first phrase. Repeat to make a second phrase of eight measures. For the last two phrases of eight measures each, play measures eleven through eighteen twice. The last time through, change the last chord in measure seventeen to E major (V^7 of A), and cadence in measure eighteen in A major. Repeat the piece as necessary.

Schumann: Drei Stücklein (Three Little Pieces), Op. 99 No. 1
4/4, MM quarter note equals 60

Use measures one through eight. In measure eight, improvise chords of appropriate E major tonality to go with the B major dominant chord at the end of measure seven. If the accompanist wishes to use the entire piece, he may play it straight through as written, which is sixteen measures. The suggestion for cadencing in measure eight will be handy if the accompanist has played the entire piece, and is going through it a second time, only to discover (as often happens) that the combination is twenty-four measures long instead of thirty-two.

Smetana: "Charming Landscape" from The Sketches, Op. 5, Book II, No. 3
2/2, MM eighth note equals 69

Play the first sixteen measures as written. The last two phrases of eight measures each will be measures seventeen through twenty-four and measures thirty-one through thirty-eight. Omit measures twenty-five through thirty. Repeat as necessary.

Music for ronds de jambe à terre

Bach: Menuet II, English Suite in F Major
3/4, MM quarter note equals 104

This piece, without repeats, totals thirty-two measures. It would be unwise to play it in this fashion, however. Measure sixteen would be halfway through the piece and is not clear and distinct harmonically as it should be to sound convincing to the dancer's ear. Therefore, it would be better to play the piece in the following manner. Play measures one through eight twice, to total sixteen measures (at measure eight, the second repeat should be taken). Then play measures nine through sixteen and skip directly to measures twenty-five through thirty-two. Measures seventeen through twenty-four are omitted. The accompanist still has four phrases of eight measures each, and the music is more harmonically convincing. Repeat as necessary.

Bach: Passepied II, Partita in B Minor (Overture in the French Manner)
⅜, MM eighth note equals 104
Play measures one through eight twice. Play measures nine through twenty-four. This makes four phrases of eight measures each. Repeat as necessary.

Beethoven: Theme and Var. I, IV, and VI from Six Variations on "Nel cor più non mi sento," *La Molinara*
⁶⁄₈, MM eighth note equals 112
The number of measures and the harmonic structures of the theme and variations I, IV, and VI are identical, and the alteration below may be applied to each individual movement. Play as written measures one through twelve. Omit measures thirteen through sixteen and go directly to measures seventeen through twenty. This makes sixteen full measures. Repeat as necessary or change to other variations.

Brahms: Waltz in E Major, Op. 39 No. 5
¾, MM quarter note equals 112
Play the opening eight measures twice. Then play from measure nine through to the end of the piece. The accompanist will be two measures short of completing four even eight-measure phrases. In other words, the last eight-measure phrase begins in measure seventeen and ends with measure twenty-two. To fill in the last two absent measures, simply repeat the last two measures (twenty-one and twenty-two), including the pickup note to measure twenty-one. This will sound natural and will square off the phrase. Repeat the piece as necessary.

Brahms: Waltz in B-Flat Major, Op. 39 No. 8
¾, MM quarter note equals 112

Play measures one through four twice, then play measures five through twelve. This makes sixteen measures. For the second sixteen measures, play measures thirteen through twenty and complete the last eight-measure phrase in the following way: play measures twenty-one through twenty-nine, omitting twenty-six and ending on twenty-nine. Examining the final phrase of the waltz, the accompanist can see that omitting measure twenty-six is the best choice, since that interferes least with the melody and phrase structure.

Chopin: Nocturne in B-Flat Minor, Op. 9 No. 1
⁶⁄₄, MM quarter note equals 116

Begin in measure nineteen, the D-flat major section. The next thirty-two measures will fall naturally into four phrases of sixteen measures each. Repeat these thirty-two measures as necessary.

Chopin: Prelude in A-Flat Major, Op. 28 No. 17
⁶⁄₈, MM eighth note equals 116

Begin with measure three and play through eighteen. This sixteen measures of ⁶⁄₈ equals thirty-two measures of ¾. Repeat as necessary.

Granados: Valses Poeticos, No. 1
¾, MM quarter note equals 116

Play the first thirty-two measures as written. If needed, play measures thirty-three through forty-eight (the remainder of the piece) twice for another thirty-two measures.

Mozart: First Movement, Sonata in A Major, Var. III and IV
⁶⁄₈, MM quarter note equals 116

For both, play measures one through sixteen as written. In measure sixteen, cadence on the last beat (A minor in Var. III and A major in Var. IV). Repeat as necessary.

Poldini: Poupée Valsante (Dancing Doll)
³⁄₈, MM eighth note equals 116

After the five-measure introduction, the following thirty-two measures fall into four equal, eight-measure phrases. Repeat as necessary.

Ravel: Menuet on the Name of Haydn
¾, MM quarter note equals 116

Play measures one through sixteen as written. In the interest of harmonic clarity, play the last two phrases of eight measures each in this way: play measures seventeen through twenty-four twice, substituting a suitable B major configuration in measure twenty-four each time. Repeat the piece as necessary.

Saint-Saëns: Valse Nonchalante, Op. 110
¾, MM quarter note equals 116

Play the first thirty-two measures as written. In measure thirty-two, cadence in D-flat major. Repeat as necessary.

Scriabin: Prelude in A Major, Op. 11 No. 7
⁶⁄₈, MM eighth note equals 116

Play the first sixteen measures and cadence on A major on the second beat of measure sixteen. Repeat as necessary. Sixteen measures of ⁶⁄₈ equals thirty-two measures of ¾.

Smetana: Chanson from Six Feuilles d'Album, Op. 2 No. 2
²⁄₄, MM quarter note equals 40

In this piece, each quarter note is subdivided into two groups of sixteenth note triplets. In this case it is very useful to change the rhythm so that the quarter note sounds as if it is divided into three groups of sixteenth note duplets. Thus each quarter note has three pulses, which resembles a ⁶⁄₈ or a ¾. This is more suitable for ronds de jambe à terre. This piece is divided into two equal sections of sixteen measures each. Each section will now appear to the dancer to be thirty-two measures of ¾ or sixteen measures of ⁶⁄₈. If the combination ends at the first sixteen measures, cadence on E minor on the second beat of measure sixteen. Repeat as necessary.

Tchaikovsky: Schneeglöckchen (Snow-Drops), Op. 37 No. 4
⁶⁄₈, MM eighth note equals 116

Play the first sixteen measures as written. Cadence in G minor in measure sixteen. For the second sixteen measures, play measures twenty-five through forty. Cadence on D minor in measure forty. Repeat as necessary.

Vogt: Twenty-four Octave Exercises, Op. 145 No. 23
⅜, MM eighth note equals 108
    This piece may be played as written. It contains four even, eight-measure phrases. Repeat as necessary.

Music for ronds de jambe en l'air

Bach: Menuet I, Partita in B-Flat Major
¾, MM dotted half note equals 60
    Use the first thirty-two measures of this movement. In measures thirty-one and thirty-two, play two measures of a B-flat cadence, instead of using what is written. This will sound rounded out and natural. Repeat the movement as necessary. The first sixteen measures may be repeated rather than continuing.

Bach: Passepied I, Partita in B Minor (Overture in the French Manner)
⅜, MM dotted eighth note equals 56
    Play this straight through without repeats. This equals thirty-two measures. Repeat the movement as necessary.

Bach: Prelude in C Major, Well-Tempered Clavier, Book I
4/4, MM half note equals 50
    There will be one ronds de jambe for each half note. The first phrase will be measures one through seven, with measure seven repeated to make eight measures. On the repeat of measure seven, play a G for the root of the arpeggio instead of B. The second phrase is measures eight through fifteen. For the third phrase, play measures sixteen through twenty-one as written, which totals six measures, and finish the last two measures as follows. In measure twenty-two use the first half note arpeggio and skip immediately to measure twenty-four, playing only the first half note arpeggio of that measure—in other words, measure seven of the third phrase consists of the first halves of measure twenty-two and measure twenty-four, combined. Use measure twenty-five to finish the third phrase. For the last phrase of eight measures, use measures twenty-six through thirty-two. Insert one mea-

sure of improvised C major arpeggios between measures twenty-eight and twenty-nine, and play a tonic C major arpeggio in measure thirty-two instead of the G⁷ arpeggio which is written.

The accompanist now has four phrases of eight measures each in which the harmonic rhythm and motion will be clear to the ear. Ironically, there are exactly thirty-two measures of music up to the point where this discussion ended. However, as written, the music does not sound like even phrases of eight measures each and therefore is not immediately usable for ballet class. The arranged version sounds quite musically acceptable if played intelligently and is a good example of the kind of thing which can be worked out with patience.

Beethoven: Bagatelles, Op. 119 No. 9
¾, MM dotted half note equals 56
    Play measures one through eight and repeat. Measures nine through twelve repeated are the third phrase of eight measures. Measures thirteen through twenty make the fourth phrase. Repeat as needed.

Brahms: Waltz in G-Sharp Minor, Op. 39 No. 3
¾, MM quarter note equals 138
    Play the piece as written. It will be sixteen or thirty-two measures, depending on whether or not the repeats are taken. Repeat as necessary.

Chopin: Etude in F Minor, Op. 10 No. 9
⁶⁄₈, MM dotted quarter note equals 56
    The tempo given above is much slower than the correct performance tempo, but for the purpose intended it is quite acceptable musically. Use the first thirty-two measures as written. In the last half of measure thirty-two, cadence in F minor. Repeat as necessary.

Czerny: The Art of Finger Dexterity, Op. 740 No. 4
⁶⁄₈, MM dotted quarter note equals 56
    The tempo given above, although much slower than the original, is very suitable in this context. Use the first sixteen measures and repeat as necessary. Cadence in B-flat major in measure sixteen.

Fauré: Berceuse, Op. 56 No. 1

²⁄₄, MM quarter note equals 52

Begin in measure three. Measures three through ten are the first phrase. Play measures eleven through fourteen twice for the second phrase of eight measures. The last time through, cadence on B major in measure fourteen. Repeat as necessary.

Schumann: "Bittendes Kind" (Entreating Child) from Kinderszenen, Op. 15 No. 4
²⁄₄, MM quarter note equals 50

Play measures one through sixteen as written. Cadence on A major on the second beat of measure sixteen. Repeat as necessary.

Schumann: Wiegenliedchen (A Little Cradle Song), Op. 124 No. 6
²⁄₄, MM quarter note equals 56

Play the first thirty-two measures as written, if needed. In measure thirty-two, cadence on D major. Repeat as necessary.

Scriabin: Etude in E Major, Op. 8 No. 5
⁴⁄₄, MM half note equals 50

The first phrase is measures one through eight. The second phrase of eight measures may be played in this way: play measures nine through twelve and then return to measures one through four. In measure four, cadence strongly on E major. Repeat as necessary.

Tchaikovsky: Chanson Triste, Op. 40 No. 2.
⁴⁄₄, MM half note equals 50

Play measures one through eight as written. For the second phrase of eight measures, proceed as follows: play measures nine through twelve, and skip immediately to measures seventeen through twenty. Repeat as necessary.

Vogt: Twenty-four Octave Studies, Op. 145 No. 7
³⁄₈, MM dotted quarter note equals 50

Play the first sixteen measures as written. Repeat this section or continue. The piece consists of three phrases of sixteen measures each. Arrange and repeat as necessary.

Music for battement tendu (quick), pas de cheval

Bach: Aria, Partita in D Major

²/₄, MM quarter note equals 60

Play the first sixteen measures as written, and repeat as necessary.

Bach: Gavotte I, Partita in B Minor (Overture in the French Manner)

²/₂, MM quarter note equals 120 (half note equals 60)

Play the entire piece as written, taking the first repeat. This is thirty-two measures of two equal sixteen-measure phrases. In listening to this movement, one would think that the first full measure of music begins with the pickup, and not where the bar line actually is. If the accompanist plays this movement as written, it will confuse the dancers. Therefore, imagine all the bar lines to be one half note in front of where they actually are. This will sound more "correct" to the dancer's ear. In playing through this Gavotte, the accompanist will be readily aware of the above problem.

Bach: Rondeau, Partita in C Minor

³/₈, MM dotted quarter note equals 60

The first sixty-four measures of this movement fall into even sixteen-measure sections, so the accompanist may play the music as written and cadence where appropriate; for instance, in C minor in measure thirty-two. Repeat as necessary.

Bartók: First Movement (Bagpipe) and Second Movement (Bear Dance) from Sonatine

²/₄, MM quarter note equals 60

In I, after the introduction of four measures, use the next sixteen measures, which are square. Repeat as necessary. In II, play measures one through eight and repeat. For the second sixteen measures, play measures nine through twelve and repeat, and then play measures thirteen through twenty. Repeat the piece as necessary.

Brahms: Variations on a Theme by Handel, Op. 24 Var. I

⁴/₄, MM quarter note equals 60

Play this variation as written (sixteen measures with repeats). The rapid thirty-second note figures may be omitted if desired. Repeat as necessary.

Dvořák: Humoreske, Op. 101 No. 7

²/₄, MM quarter note equals 60

Play the first eight measures as written. For the second phrase, play measures nine through twelve and repeat. Repeat the entire section (sixteen measures) as necessary.

Satie: Les Pantins Dansent
²/₄, MM half note equals 56
  Play the first sixty-four measures as needed, and repeat if necessary. This piece falls into even sixteen-measure sections, and an improvised cadence at any phrase ending is no problem.

Scharwenka: March, Op. 62 No. 1
⁴/₄, MM half note equals 60
  This entire piece falls into distinct eight-measure phrases. Play as necessary.

Schubert: Impromptu, Op. 142 No. 3
⁴/₄, MM quarter note equals 60
  Play the first sixteen measures as written, and repeat as necessary.

Schubert: Sechs Ecossaisen, D. 421, Nos. 1, 2, 3, and 5
²/₄, MM quarter note equals 66
  Each piece is sixteen measures long. Play and repeat as necessary.

Schumann: "Armes Waisenkind" (Poor Orphan) from Album for the Young, Op. 68
²/₄, MM quarter note equals 56
  This piece is thirty-two measures of even phrases. Play and repeat as necessary.

Vogt: Twenty-four Octave Studies, Op. 145 No. 6
²/₄, MM quarter note equals 54
  This exercise consists of two even sections of sixteen measures each. Play and repeat as necessary.

Music for battement tendu dégagé, battement frappé

Bach: Bourée I, Partita in B Minor (Overture in the French Manner)
²/₂, MM half note equals 88
  Measures one through four repeated are the first phrase. Mea-

sures five through twelve are the second phrase. Measures thirteen through sixteen, repeated, are the third phrase. (The first time measure sixteen is played, two A-minor chords are sufficient; this sounds smoother and clearer, harmonically. The second time through measure sixteen, play as written, and proceed to the fourth phrase.) Phrase four is measures seventeen through twenty-four. Repeat the piece as necessary.

Bach: Bourée II, Partita in B Minor
2/2, MM half note equals 88

The first phrase of eight measures is measures one through four repeated. Phrase two is measures five through twelve. The third and fourth phrases are measures thirteen through twenty-eight as written. Repeat as necessary.

Bach: Echo, Partita in B Minor
2/4, MM quarter note equals 96

Use only the first sixteen measures of this piece, as the measures which follow may lead to confusion. Repeat the first sixteen measures as necessary, cadencing in F-sharp minor in measure sixteen.

Bartók: Peasant Dance from Mikrokosmos, Vol. V No. 128
2/4, MM quarter note equals 100

The first four measures are introductory. Play measures five through twenty for the first two phrases of eight measures each. If stopping in measure twenty, cadence on a strong E flat. Repeat as necessary. This piece would not be useful after measure twenty.

Brahms: Variations on a Theme by Paganini, Op. 35, Book II, Var. III
2/4, MM quarter note equals 92

Play this variation straight through without repeats, a total of sixteen measures. Then repeat as necessary.

Liszt: Hungarian Rhapsody No. 6
2/4, MM quarter note equals 96

Begin in measure ninety-six, which is the opening of the B-flat major section. Play the first sixteen measures of the theme as written. For the second sixteen measures, play the next eight measures and repeat them, ending in the last measure (119) on D major. Repeat the whole section as necessary.

Satie: La Diva de l'Empire
²/₄, MM quarter note equals 88

Begin in measure nine. The following sixty-four measures fall
into even phrases, so the accompanist may use and repeat whatever
amount of music is necessary.

Schubert: Acht Ecossaisen, D. 529
²/₄, MM half note equals 92

Numbers 1 through 4 and 6 through 8 are sixteen measures long.
Play and repeat as necessary. Number 5 is twenty-four measures long,
so the last eight measures may be repeated.

Schubert: Moment Musical, Op. 94 No. 3
²/₄, MM quarter note equals 92

After two introductory measures, the next thirty-two measures
are square. The last eight measures of the piece may also be used.
Except for measures thirty-five through forty-four, which is a phrase
of ten measures, the other sections may be played as written and
combined in any fashion desired.

Schumann: Nachtstücke, Op. 23 No. 1
⁴/₄, MM quarter note equals 96

The first sixteen measures of this piece are sufficient. In measure
sixteen, cadence on a strong E-minor chord on beat three. If repeating
and going back to the beginning, play measure sixteen as written.

Schumann: Scherzino from Faschingsschwank aus Wien, Op. 26
²/₄, MM quarter note equals 100

Use the first sixteen or thirty-two measures. In measure thirty-
two, cadence on a strong A-flat major chord. Repeat as necessary.

Tchaikovsky: Humoresque, Op. 10 No. 2
²/₄, MM quarter note equals 96

The first phrase begins in measure ten. The following thirty-two
measures are comprised of four even phrases of eight measures each.
Beginning in measure forty-two (the E-flat section), the next sixteen
measures may be used and repeated as necessary. The opening G
major section and the second E-flat major section may be used sepa-
rately for different combinations.

Vogt: Twenty-four Octave Studies, Op. 145 No. 2
2/4, MM quarter note equals 100

The first sixteen measures may be played as written. For a second sixteen-measure section, play measures seventeen through twenty-four twice. The second time through these measures, cadence on A minor on the second beat of measure twenty-four. Repeat the entire section as necessary.

Music for battement sur le cou-de-pied, pointé

Bartók: Third Movement (Finale) from Sonatine
2/4, MM quarter note equals 120

Begin in measure five, and include the pickup from measure four. Use measures five through twenty, and repeat as necessary. Repeated once, this equals thirty-two measures. When ending in measure twenty, cadence on a strong G-major chord.

Beethoven: Rondo a Capriccio, Op. 129
2/4, MM quarter note equals 144

Play the first sixteen measures as written. Measures seventeen through twenty-four played twice may be used for a second sixteen measures. Measures twenty-five through forty may be used for another sixteen-measure phrase if needed, and then repeated, if necessary, to make a full sixty-four measures of music.

Brahms: Variations on a Theme by Handel, Op. 24 Var. VII
4/4, MM quarter note equals 112

Play this variation as written (sixteen measures with repeats). Repeat as necessary, and cadence on B-flat major on the third beat of measure eight the last time through. If the dance combination happens to be an uneven one and ends on measure four the second time through, then cadence on F major on the third beat.

Burgmuller: L'Hirondelle (The Swallow)
4/4, MM quarter note equals 132

Use measures one through sixteen, and repeat if necessary. Cadence in D major in measure sixteen.

Chopin: Etude in A Minor, Op. 25 No. 4
4/4, MM quarter note equals 132

Use the first sixteen measures of this etude, and repeat if necessary. In measure sixteen, cadence on E minor on the third beat.

Czerny: The Art of Finger Dexterity, Op. 740 No. 7
4/4, MM quarter note equals 132
   Use the first sixteen measures of this exercise as written, and repeat as necessary.

Czerny: The Art of Finger Dexterity, Op. 740 No. 9
2/4, MM quarter note equals 132
   Use the first sixteen or thirty-two measures as written, repeating as necessary. In measure thirty-two, end on B major (as a tonic); or, if repeating and going back to the beginning, play as written (B major V^7 of E major).

Czerny: The Art of Finger Dexterity, Op. 740 No. 11
4/4, MM quarter note equals 126
   Use measures one through sixteen as written, and repeat as necessary.

Czerny: The Art of Finger Dexterity, Op. 740 No. 30
2/4, MM quarter note equals 126
   Use the first sixteen or thirty-two measures, repeating as necessary. If ending with measure thirty-two, cadence on C major.

Mozart: Third Movement (Rondo), Sonata in A Major
2/4, MM quarter note equals 126
   Play measures one through eight twice. Measures nine through twenty-four are the second sixteen-measure phrase. If more music is needed, play measures twenty-five through thirty-two twice for a third phrase, and go back to the beginning and play measures one through eight twice to make the fourth phrase.

Rodgers (Richard): "The Sweetest Sounds" from *No Strings*
2/4, MM quarter note equals 120
   Use the first thirty-two measures of this refrain. Cadence on a strong B-flat major in measure thirty-two. Repeat as necessary.

Schumann: "Wilder Reiter" (Wild Rider) from Album for the Young,

Op. 68
⁶/₈, MM dotted quarter note equals 126
   Play measures one through eight twice. Then play the remainder of the piece, which is sixteen additional measures. Repeat as necessary.

Music for battement en cloche

Beethoven: Theme from Variations on a Waltz by Diabelli, Op. 120
¾, MM dotted half note equals 69
   The theme is divided into two phrases of sixteen measures each. Play and repeat as necessary.

Brahms: Waltz in B Major, Op. 39 No. 1
¾, MM dotted half note equals 63
   Play the first eight measures and repeat, then play the last sixteen measures of the waltz. Play and repeat as necessary.

Brahms: Variations on a Theme by Paganini, Op. 35, Book I, Var. VIII
⁶/₈, MM dotted quarter note equals 66
   Play this variation straight through (sixteen measures) and repeat as necessary. When ending in measure sixteen, cadence on a strong A-minor chord on the second beat.

Schubert: Twelve Valses Nobles, Op. 77, D. 969, No. 1, 2, and 3
¾, MM dotted half note equals 66
   Play the first sixteen or thirty-two measures of any of these waltzes. They are all square and clear-cut, harmonically. Repeat as necessary.

Schumann: Marche des Davidsbündler Contre les Philistins from Carnaval, Op. 9
¾, MM dotted half note equals 54
   Play the first eight measures and repeat. Then play the last sixteen measures. This totals thirty-two measures. Use only the first ending (measures twenty-two through twenty-four), cadencing in a clear F minor.

Schumann: Arlequin from Carnaval, Op. 9
¾, MM dotted half note equals 66
   Play measures one through sixteen as written. Then play mea-

sures seventeen through twenty-four twice. This totals thirty-two measures. Whether ending in measure sixteen or in measure twenty-four, finish with a strong B-flat major cadence.

Vogt: Twenty-four Octave Studies, Op. 145 No. 12
6/8, MM dotted eighth note equals 66
    Play the first sixteen or thirty-two measures as needed, and repeat if necessary.

Music for grand battement

Beethoven: Variations on a Waltz by Diabelli, Op. 120 Var. I
4/4, MM whole note equals 63
    Play this piece straight through to sixteen or thirty-two measures. Repeat as needed. If ending in measure sixteen, cadence on a strong G major.

Bizet: "Toreador Song" from *Carmen*
2/4, MM half note equals 60
    The main theme from the "Toreador Song" (the first sixteen measures) is often useful for grand battement. Repeat as necessary.

Brahms: Variations on a Theme by Handel, Op. 24 Var. XXV
4/4, MM quarter note equals 69
    Play this variation straight through and repeat as necessary. The accompanist may provide a stronger beat by playing the first sixteenth note of each bass figure on the beat, rather than one sixteenth note off the beat, as written. The second sixteenth note of each bass figure may remain as written, on the "and" of each beat.

Brahms: Variations on a Theme by Paganini, Op. 35, Book I, Var. XIII
2/4, MM quarter note equals 69
    Play this variation with the first repeat. This will total sixteen measures. Repeat the variation as necessary.

Fauré: Theme (Quasi Adagio) from Theme and Variations, Op. 73
4/4, MM quarter note equals 60
    Omit measures five through eight. The first phrase of eight measures is measures one through four and nine through twelve. The second phrase is measures thirteen through twenty. Repeat as necessary.

Grieg: Wedding-Day at Troldhaugen, Op. 65 No. 6
4/4, MM half note equals 60

There is an introduction of two measures. The first phrase of eight measures is measures three through ten. Omit measures eleven and twelve. The second phrase is measures thirteen through twenty. Repeat these two phrases as necessary. Cadence on a strong, full D-major chord.

Liszt: Etude No. 6, Var. III from Six Paganini Etudes
2/4, MM quarter note equals 69

Play this variation as written (sixteen measures) and repeat if necessary.

Liszt: Opening Theme from Hungarian Rhapsody No. 6
2/4, MM quarter note equals 60

Measures one through four are introductory. Use measures five through twenty (sixteen measures). Measures twenty-one through thirty-six may also be used for another sixteen-measure phrase. If ending at measure thirty-six, play a strong cadence on D-flat major, rather than as written. Repeat as necessary.

Prokofiev: March from *Love of Three Oranges*
4/4, MM half note equals 60

The first phrase begins in measure three and ends at ten. The second phrase is measures eleven through eighteen. Repeat as necessary or cadence in measure eighteen on C minor, the third beat.

Vogt: Twenty-four Octave Studies, Op. 145 No. 15
2/4, MM quarter note equals 60

Play the first eight measures and repeat. For the second phrase of sixteen measures, play measures nine through twelve and repeat, then play measures thirteen through twenty. Repeat the exercise as necessary.

The Center

Music for adagio (attitudes, arabesques, other posés; promenade; temps lié)

Bach: Sarabande, French Suite No. 1
¾, MM quarter note equals 72

Play the first eight measures and repeat. Then play measures nine through twenty-four. This totals thirty-two measures. Repeat as necessary.

Beethoven: Second Movement from Sonata *(Pathétique)*, Op. 13
²/₄, MM eighth note equals 60

Play the first sixteen measures as written. For an additional sixteen measures to complete the combination, the best possibility is probably measures fifty-one through sixty-six. Cadence in A-flat major in measure sixty-six. Repeat this music as necessary.

Brahms: Intermezzo, Op. 119 No. 2
¾, MM quarter note equals 104

Begin in measure thirty-six, the opening of the E-major section. Use the first thirty-two measures of this section, repeating as necessary.

Brahms: Variations on a Theme by Paganini, Op. 35, Book II, Var. XII
⁶/₈, MM eighth note equals 104

Play this entire variation, taking only the first repeat. This totals sixteen measures. Repeat as necessary.

Chopin: Etude, Op. 25 No. 5
¾, MM quarter note equals 138

Begin in the E-major section (piu lento). Play the first sixteen measures as written. The next phrase of sixteen measures may be arranged as follows: play measures seventeen through twenty-eight and skip immediately to measures thirty-three through thirty-six. One may cadence at the end of measure thirty-six, or if more than thirty-two measures of music is required, the accompanist may repeat the entire section. Instead of repeating, he may elect to play measures thirty-seven through fifty-two and repeat this much music for an additional sixteen or thirty-two measures.

Chopin: Prelude, Op. 28 No. 15
⁴/₄, MM quarter note equals 66

Measures one through eight are the first phrase. Phrase two is measures nine through twelve played twice. The third phrase is measures thirteen through nineteen (measure nineteen is played twice). The last phrase is measures twenty through twenty-seven. Repeat the entire section as necessary.

Chopin: Funeral March from Sonata in B-Flat Minor, Op. 35
4/4, MM quarter note equals 60

Use the middle section of the Funeral March, which begins in D-flat major. Use this entire section, taking only the first repeat. This totals thirty-two measures. Repeat as necessary.

Glazunov: Barcarolle from *The Seasons*
6/8, MM eighth note equals 116

The opening eight measures are introductory. Begin with measure nine, and use the following thirty-two measures as written. In the last measure (forty), cadence on E-flat major on the second beat.

Liszt: Consolations, No. 2
4/4, MM quarter note equals 116

Play the first sixteen measures as written. For the second phrase, play measures seventeen through twenty-four twice. Repeat as necessary.

Mozart: Second Movement from Sonata in F Major, K. 332
4/4, MM eighth note equals 76

If the combination is not too heavy, this material is refreshing in its purity and simplicity. Measures one through eight will be sufficient. Cadence in F major in measure eight, or if repeating, make the last beat in measure eight an F^7, in preparation for the opening in B-flat major.

Puccini: "Oh! mio babbino caro" (Oh! my beloved daddy) from *Gianni Schicchi*
6/8, MM eighth note equals 112

Play measures one through sixteen as written. For the second sixteen measures, play measures seventeen through twenty-four, repeat measures seventeen through twenty-two, and then skip to measures twenty-five and twenty-six. The above process will result in a logical sequence of thirty-two measures. Repeat as necessary.

Rachmaninoff: Piano Concerto No. 1, Op. 1
4/4, MM quarter note equals 63

Begin in measure one hundred seventy-two (use the pickup from the preceding measure). Use measures one hundred seventy-two through one hundred seventy-nine. This may easily be repeated as needed. When ending in measure one hundred seventy-nine, resolve the C-sharp[7] to a strong F-sharp minor chord.

Rachmaninoff: Prelude, Op. 23 No. 4
¾, MM quarter note equals 66

The first two measures are introductory. Begin in measure three. Use the following thirty-two measures as written, repeating as necessary. At the end of the thirty-two measure section cadence in D major.

Rachmaninoff: Prelude, Op. 23 No. 5
4/4, MM quarter note equals 66

Begin in measure thirty-five, the middle section of this prelude. The first phrase is measures one through seven, playing measure seven twice. For the second phrase, play measures eight through fifteen and cadence in D major (or repeat if necessary).

Rachmaninoff: Prelude, Op. 23 No. 6
4/4, MM quarter note equals 72

The phrase begins with measure two, ending on measure nine. One may incorporate the pickup from measure one into the introduction. For the second phrase, skip directly (and smoothly, to make it sound natural) to measures sixteen through twenty-three. One may cadence in measure twenty-three on E-flat major. This whole section may be repeated, or measures twenty-four through thirty-nine may be played as written to fill out another sixteen measures. One may play a strong E-flat major cadence in measure thirty-nine if ending at that point.

Ravel: Waltz No. 2 in G Minor, Valses Nobles et Sentimentales
¾, MM quarter note equals 88

This piece falls into four equal sections of sixteen measures each, so no alterations are necessary.

Rimsky-Korsakov: "A Flight of Passing Clouds," Op. 24 No. 3
12/8, MM dotted quarter note equals 48

This is a song, so the score is piano-vocal. The accompanist should be able to arrange the accompaniment and melody in order to use it for ballet. Besides playing the melody, the right hand may fill in the harmonic texture, in order to ease the burden of the left hand. The first measure is introductory. Measures two through nine are the first phrase. Omit measure ten. For the second phrase of eight measures, use measures eleven through eighteen. In measure eighteen, improvise a C-sharp[7] (V[7] of F-sharp minor) arpeggio for the first two beats, and fill out the last two beats of the measure with a strong F-sharp minor tonality. Repeat the entire piece as needed.

Scriabin: Prelude, Op. 11 No. 11
⁶/₈, MM eighth note equals 126
The first sixteen or thirty-two measures of this prelude may be used. If ending in measure sixteen, one may cadence on D-sharp minor on the second beat. If ending in measure thirty-two, one may cadence on a full B-major chord on the second beat.

Music for slow pirouettes from 4th, 5th, 2nd

Brahms: Waltz in B Major, Op. 39 No. 13
¾, MM quarter note equals 138
Play this waltz as written (sixteen measures without repeats). Repeat as necessary.

Brahms: Waltz in A-Flat Major, Op. 39 No. 15
¾, MM quarter note equals 126
Play measures one through eight and repeat. For the next sixteen measures, play measures nine through twenty-two. Measures thirteen and fourteen must be repeated to round out the first eight-measure phrase of this second section. The above process makes a total of thirty-two measures. Repeat as necessary, or play a full A-flat cadence in measure twenty-two.

Chopin: Waltz, Op. 69 No. 1
¾, MM quarter note equals 126
The first sixty-four measures will be adequate, being comprised of even phrases of eight and sixteen measures. Repeat as necessary.

Chopin: Waltz, Op. 70 No. 2

¾, MM quarter note equals 132

Play the first sixteen measures as written. Omit measures seventeen through twenty. The second sixteen measures are twenty-one through thirty-six. Cadence in E-flat major in measure thirty-six. Repeat as necessary.

Delibes: Valse from Act I of *Coppelia*
¾, MM quarter note equals 126

Begin with measure five. Use the following thirty-two measures as written, and repeat as necessary.

Granados: Valses Poeticos, No. 2
¾, MM quarter note equals 138

Use the first thirty-two measures of this waltz and repeat as necessary.

Liszt: Opening Theme from Hungarian Rhapsody No. 6
²⁄₄, MM quarter note equals 42

Measures one through four are introductory. Use measures five through twenty (sixteen measures). Measures twenty-one through thirty-six may also be used for another sixteen-measure phrase. If ending at measure thirty-six, play a strong cadence on D-flat major, rather than as written. Repeat as necessary. Although generally a slow or moderate ¾ is used for this exercise, a ²⁄₄ like the one above sometimes works quite well.

Schubert: Twenty Waltzes, Op. 127, D. 146, Nos. 17 and 18
¾, MM quarter note equals 126

Each waltz has sixteen measures. Play and repeat as necessary.

Schumann: Promenade from Carnaval, Op. 9
¾, MM quarter note equals 138

Use the first thirty-two measures as written, and repeat as necessary.

Schumann: Valse Noble from Carnaval, Op. 9
¾, MM quarter note equals 138

Play measures one through sixteen (taking no repeats). Omit measures seventeen through twenty-four. For the second phrase of sixteen measures, play measures twenty-five through forty. Repeat as necessary.

Music for petit allegro (²⁄₄)

Since a ⁶⁄₈ meter is often as good as a ²⁄₄ or ⁴⁄₄ meter (providing it is sharp and bright), a tarantella (which is a bright ⁶⁄₈, MM dotted quarter note equals 104) is often good for petit allegro steps. The accompanist is encouraged to locate several of these Italian character pieces to have on hand.

Chopin: Etude, Op. 10 No. 5
²⁄₄, MM quarter note equals 100
Use the first sixteen measures of this etude. In measure sixteen, cadence on G-flat major on the second beat. Repeat as necessary.

Chopin: Etude, Op. 25 No. 9
²⁄₄, MM quarter note equals 104
Use the first sixteen measures as written, and repeat as necessary. In measure sixteen, cadence on a strong D-flat major chord on the second beat.

Czerny: The Art of Finger Dexterity, Op. 740 No. 29
²⁄₄, MM quarter note equals 100
Begin in measure fifty-six. Use the following sixteen measures (fifty-six through seventy-one). Measure seventy-one should be on a strong D-major cadence. Repeat as necessary.

Czerny: The Art of Finger Dexterity, Op. 740 No. 33
⁶⁄₈, MM dotted quarter note equals 96
Use the first thirty-two measures of this exercise. Measure thirty-two should be replaced with a strong E-flat major cadence. Prepare this by playing a strong B-flat⁷ chord in measure thirty-two, beat one. Repeat the exercise as necessary.

Czerny: The Art of Finger Dexterity, Op. 740 No. 35
²⁄₄, MM quarter note equals 84
Use the first thirty-two measures as written. Cadence in measure sixteen or measure thirty-two, repeating as necessary.

Czerny: The Art of Finger Dexterity, Op. 740 No. 44
²/₄, MM quarter note equals 88

Begin in measure forty-four and use the following thirty-two measures, ending with measure seventy-five. Cadence on a strong G-major chord in measure seventy-five. Repeat as necessary.

Czerny: The Art of Finger Dexterity, Op. 740 No. 47
²/₄, MM quarter note equals 76

Use the first thirty-two measures as written. Cadence as the harmony indicates, and repeat as necessary.

Debussy: "Golliwogg's Cake Walk" from Children's Corner
²/₄, MM quarter note equals 92

Begin in measure ten, and use the following thirty-two measures. Cadence on a strong E-flat major chord in measure forty-one. Repeat as necessary.

Dvořák: Slavonic Dance No. 2
²/₄, MM quarter note equals 92

Play measures one through sixteen as written. Then play measures seventeen through twenty-four twice for the second sixteen measures. Repeat as necessary. Play this entire section in the same bright tempo, disregarding sudden tempo changes in the score.

Gershwin: Prelude No. 3
²/₄, MM quarter note equals 100

Begin with measure five. Use measures five through twenty, and repeat as necessary. In measure twenty, cadence on a strong E-flat major chord.

Grieg: Album Leaf, Op. 12 No. 7
²/₄, MM quarter note equals 88

Use measures one through sixteen, repeating as necessary. Cadence in measure sixteen in B-minor, with a strong F-sharp[7] major chord in measure fifteen. Play this staccato and bright, not slurred.

Schubert: Nine Ecossaises from Op. 18, D. 145
²/₄, MM quarter note equals 92

All of these pieces are in clear, eight-measure phrases. Play and repeat them as necessary.

Schubert: Galop and Eight Ecossaises, Op. 49, D. 735
2/4, MM quarter note equals 88

 All of these pieces, also, are in clear, eight-measure phrases. Play and repeat as necessary.

Schumann: Aveu from Carnaval, Op. 9
2/4, MM quarter note equals 104

 Play the first four measures and repeat, then play measures five through twelve. This totals sixteen measures. Repeat as necessary.

Schumann: Reconnaissance from Carnaval, Op. 9
2/4, MM quarter note equals 88

 Use the first sixteen measures, repeating as necessary. In measure sixteen, cadence on a strong A-flat major chord.

Schumann: Davidsbündlertänze, No. 12
2/4, MM quarter note equals 92

 Use the first sixteen measures, cadencing on a solid E-major chord in measure sixteen. Repeat as necessary.

Music for petit allegro (¾)

Chopin: Waltz, Op. 64 No. 3
¾, MM dotted half note equals 80

 Use the first thirty-two measures of this waltz, and repeat as necessary. Cadence on a strong E-flat major chord in measure thirty-two.

Chopin: Waltz, Op. 70 No. 1
¾, MM dotted half note equals 80

 Use the first thirty-two measures, and repeat as necessary. Cadence as appropriate.

Delibes: Valse de la Poupée from Act II of *Coppelia*
¾, MM dotted half note equals 66

 Begin in measure nine of the ¾, using the pickup from measure eight. Use the following thirty-two measures and repeat as necessary.

Granados: Valses Poeticos, Nos. 4 and 6
¾, MM dotted half note equals 66

The fourth waltz is thirty-two measures. Play and repeat as necessary. Use the first thirty-two measures of the sixth waltz and cadence as appropriate. Repeat as necessary.

Porter (Cole): "True Love" from *High Society*
¾, MM dotted half note equals 66
    This refrain is thirty-two measures long. Play and repeat as necessary. The tempo is somewhat faster than in the original, and this changes the mood, making a suitable light waltz.

Ravel: Waltz No. 3 in G Major, Valses Nobles et Sentimentales
¾, MM dotted half note equals 72
    Play the first sixteen measures as written. Play measures seventeen through twenty-four twice. This totals thirty-two measures. When ending in measure twenty-four, cadence on a strong D-major chord.

Schubert: As stated in the introduction to this chapter, there are dozens of Schubert waltzes which could be used here. Two specific examples which are representative of this style are given below. The accompanist may collect and use many more of these waltzes if he desires.

Schubert: Twelve Valses Nobles, Op. 77, D. 969, No. 2
¾, MM dotted half note equals 76
    Play this piece straight through (thirty-two measures) and repeat as necessary.

Schubert: Twelve Valses Nobles, Op. 77, D. 969, No. 3
¾, MM dotted half note equals 76
    Play the first thirty-two measures of this waltz as written. If more music is desired, repeat or do as follows: play measures thirty-three through forty-eight and measures fifty-three through sixty-eight (omit measures forty-nine through fifty-two).

Tchaikovsky: Tempo di Valse from Weihnachten (December), Op. 37 No. 12
¾, MM dotted half note equals 80
    Play measures one through sixteen as written. For a second phrase of sixteen measures, do as follows: play measures seventeen

through thirty as written, and improvise one bar of G⁷ leading to a final C-major bar for the closing two measures. Repeat as necessary.

Vogt: Twenty-four Octave Studies, Op. 145 No. 8
¾, MM dotted half note equals 80
   Play the first thirty-two measures as written, and repeat as necessary.

Music for grand allegro (¾)

Brahms: Waltz in B Major, Op. 39 No. 1
¾, MM dotted half note equals 63
   Play this waltz as written, taking only the first repeat. This totals thirty-two measures. Repeat as necessary.

Brahms: Waltz in G Major, Op. 39 No. 10
¾, MM dotted half note equals 63
   Play this waltz with all repeats (thirty-two measures). Repeat as necessary.

Brahms: Waltz in B Minor, Op. 39 No. 11
¾, MM dotted half note equals 63
   Play the first sixteen measures and repeat. For another thirty-two measures of music, play measures seventeen through thirty-two as written, then play measures thirty-three through forty twice. Repeat this piece as necessary (sixty-four measures).

Chopin: Waltz, Op. 18
¾, MM dotted half note equals 69
   Play the score energetically and strongly throughout. The first four measures are introductory. Use the next eighty measures, and repeat as necessary. (Eighty measures is five phrases of sixteen measures each.)

Chopin: Waltz, Op. 34 No. 1
¾, MM dotted half note equals 69
   Begin with measure seventeen. Use the next sixty-four measures and repeat as necessary.

Chopin: Waltz, Op. 42

¾, MM dotted half note equals 69

Begin with measure nine. Use the following sixty-four measures and repeat as necessary.

Chopin: Waltz, Op. 64 No. 2
¾, MM dotted half note equals 63

Use the first thirty-two measures. The second section of this waltz, which has a smoother, more running character, will not be suitable for many combinations with big leaps. However, for fast waltzes which stay closer to the floor, this section may be suitable.

Glazunov: Entrée from *Raymonda*
⁶/₈, MM dotted quarter note equals 63

Begin with measure thirty-five (tempo di valse). Use the following sixteen measures (which equal thirty-two measures of ¾) and repeat as necessary.

Glazunov: Valse des Bluets et des Pavots from *The Seasons*
¾, MM dotted half note equals 63

Measures one through four are introductory. Use the following ninety-six measures, and repeat as necessary (six phrases of sixteen measures each.

Granados: Valses Poeticos, No. 5
¾, MM dotted half note equals 66

Measures one and two are introductory. Use measures three through twenty-six (twenty-four measures), repeating the last eight measures. This totals thirty-two measures. Repeat as necessary.

Minkus: Pas de Deux from *Don Quixote*
¾, MM dotted half note equals 63

Begin with the tempo di valse in measure seventeen. Play the entire waltz (forty-eight measures) and repeat as necessary. This is an excellent example of a grand allegro waltz, and the accompanist should strive to achieve a similar feeling in other waltzes which he uses for grand allegro.

Rodgers (Richard): "Lover" from *Love Me Tonight*
¾, MM dotted half note equals 66

Measure one is where the words begin. Use all sixty-four measures of this waltz as needed. It breaks down into four phrases of sixteen measures each. Repeat as necessary.

Rox (John): "It's a Big Wide Wonderful World"
¾, MM dotted half note equals 66
Use all sixty-four measures of this waltz as needed, and repeat as necessary.

Schubert: Waltzes, Op. 9, D. 365, Nos. 1, 12, and 13
¾, MM dotted half note equals 63
Each waltz is sixteen measures long and has repeats. Play and repeat as necessary. They may be combined. Play strongly and energetically.

Schubert: Twelve Valses Nobles, Op. 77, D. 969, No. 4
¾, MM dotted half note equals 69
Play all forty-eight measures as written, repeating as necessary. Play strongly and energetically throughout, using octaves in the left hand on the first beat of each measure. A stronger lift will be implied if the rhythm in the right hand of measure one (and all other measures with the same rhythm) is changed from ♩. ♪ ♩ to ♩ ♩. ♪ . This latter rhythm is characteristic of many grand allegro waltzes and should be employed whenever possible and convenient.

Schubert: Twelve Valses Nobles, Op. 77, D. 969, No. 9
¾, MM dotted half note equals 66
Play measures one through sixteen as written. For another phrase of sixteen measures, play measures seventeen through twenty-eight, repeating measures twenty-five through twenty-eight. Repeat as necessary. The right-hand rhythm may again be changed from ♩. ♪ ♫ or ♩ ♩ ♩ to ♩ ♩. ♪ to provide more lift.

Schumann: Valse Allemande from Carnaval, Op. 9
¾, MM dotted half note equals 63
Play the piece through, taking only the first repeat. This totals thirty-two measures. Repeat as necessary. Play strongly throughout.

Schumann: Waltz, Op. 124 No. 4

¾, MM dotted half note equals 66

Play measures one through sixteen. For the second phrase of sixteen measures, play measures seventeen through twenty and repeat, followed by measures twenty-one through twenty-eight. Octaves should be used for the first beat of the left hand in each measure. This waltz uses the motive mentioned above, which is very effective in grand allegro waltzes (for example, measure four: ♪ ♩. ♪). It falls, however, on an even-numbered measure rather than on the more desirable odd-numbered one.

Music for pas de basque

¾, MM quarter note equals 72-104

This step was described as a slower ¾, with three distinct beats. Suitable music would be a slow, stately mazurka or a moderate polonaise. Use a polonaise for the slower tempos and a stately mazurka for the faster tempos. If the tempo is a slow one, a mazurka will sound too dragging. Although many mazurkas (for instance, a large number of those by Chopin) will be too fast to be suitable, they will be very appropriate for faster combinations on many occasions (petit allegro ¾), and the accompanist is advised to have on hand a stock of mazurkas in varying styles (including some of Chopin).

Chopin: Mazurka in G Minor, Op. 24 No. 1
¾, MM quarter note equals 104

Play the first thirty-two measures as written, and repeat as necessary.

Chopin: Polonaise, Op. 40 No. 1
¾, MM quarter note equals 76

Play the first fifty-six measures as written (measures one through eight should be played twice). Repeat as necessary.

Chopin: Polonaise, Op. 40 No. 2
¾, MM quarter note equals 72

Begin in measure three. Use the following thirty-two measures and repeat as necessary.

Chopin: Polonaise, Op. 44
¾, MM quarter note equals 80

Begin with measure nine. Use measures nine through twenty-six (omit measures nineteen and twenty to make the phrase square). Repeat as necessary.

Delibes: Mazurka from Act I of *Coppelia*
¾, MM quarter note equals 104

Use measures one through thirty-two (do not count the opening measure with the tremolo and scale), and repeat as necessary.

Delibes: Bolero from Act II of *Coppelia*
⅜, MM eighth note equals 104

Begin with measure ten. Use measures ten through twenty-five (sixteen measures). Repeat as necessary. Measures thirty-six through sixty-seven (thirty-two measures) may also be used. If ending in measure sixty-seven, cadence on a strong B-major chord. Repeat as necessary.

Liszt: Polonaise in E Major, No. 2
¾, MM quarter note equals 72

Begin with measure six. Use measures six through twenty-one (sixteen measures). Measures twenty-two through thirty-seven may also be used. When ending with measure thirty-seven, cadence in B major. Prepare for this by playing B major on beat two of measure thirty-six, and F-sharp major V^7 on the third beat. This will steer the harmony clearly to the B-major cadence.

Scharwenka: Polish Dance
¾, MM quarter note equals 104 (considerably slower than the original tempo, but suitable for the purpose intended)

Use the first forty-eight measures as written, and repeat as necessary. Make the left hand sharp and accented, to increase the feeling of vitality.

Music for relevés and sous-sus

Sometimes during the grand allegro work, the female dancers will put on their pointe shoes (if they are not already wearing them). Since they may warm up their feet by doing relevés or sous-sus, music for these steps will be inserted at this point. Besides the music suggested below, many of the petit allegro ²⁄₄ pieces previously mentioned may be used here with a somewhat slower tempo. In addition, much of the bright ²/₄ and ⁴/₄ music from the barre work would be suitable.

Delibes: Thème Slave Varié from Act I of *Coppelia*
²/₄, MM quarter note equals 76
    Begin with measure three and use the following twenty-four measures. Repeat the last eight measures (nineteen through twenty-six). This totals thirty-two measures. Repeat as necessary.

Delibes: Gigue from Act II of *Coppelia*
²/₄, MM quarter note equals 84
    Begin with measure nine. This piece falls into consecutive eight-measure sections. Play and repeat as necessary.

Delibes: Marche des Guerrières from Act III of *Coppelia*
²/₄, MM quarter note equals 69
    Begin with measure three and use the following thirty-two measures, repeating if necessary.

Delibes: Dance de Fête from Act III of *Coppelia*
²/₄, MM quarter note equals 72
    Begin with measure eight and use the following sixteen measures. Repeat as necessary.

Gershwin (George): "Fascinating Rhythm" from *Lady Be Good*
⁴/₄, MM half note equals 72
    Measure one is where the words begin. Use sixteen measures or all thirty-two if needed. Repeat as necessary. If cadencing in measure sixteen, prepare the E-flat resolution with a strong B-flat major V^7 chord in measure fifteen.

Glazunov: Variation II from *Raymonda*
²/₄, MM quarter note equals 72
    Begin with measure three. Use the following thirty-two measures, and repeat as necessary.

Schubert: Military March, Op. 51 No. 1
²/₄, MM quarter note equals 84
    Begin with measure seven. Use the following sixteen measures

(seven through twenty-two). Repeat as necessary.

Music for grand allegro (²/₄), fast pirouettes in place and moving

Besides the music listed below, the accompanist is encouraged to collect numerous pieces from the following categories: cancans, polkas, krakoviaks (Polish), galops, and codas from various ballet scores such as the *Nutcracker* and *Swan Lake*. These kinds of pieces are ideal for grand allegro ²/₄ steps and for fast pirouettes.

Brahms: Hungarian Dance No. 5
²/₄, MM quarter note equals 138
Play the first forty-eight measures as written, and repeat as necessary.

Delibes: Czardas from Act I of *Coppelia*
²/₄, MM quarter note equals 144
Begin with measure eighty-two (plus animé). Use the first forty-eight measures of this section, plus the final section of the czardas (marked presto) for another sixteen measures. Play in a uniform tempo throughout, and repeat as necessary.

Delibes: Galop Final from Act III of *Coppelia*
²/₄, MM quarter note equals 138
Begin with measure seven. Play the following thirty-two measures as written. Play the next sixteen measures (forty through fifty-five) twice for another section of thirty-two measures. Repeat the piece as necessary.

Glazunov: Coda from *Raymonda*
²/₄, MM quarter note equals 132
Use as much of this coda as needed, and repeat as necessary. It falls into consecutive sixteen-measure sections.

Glazunov: Galop from *Raymonda*
²/₄, MM quarter note equals 132
Use as much as desired, and repeat as necessary. This galop falls into consecutive sixteen-measure sections.

Liszt: Hungarian Rhapsody No. 2
²/₄, MM quarter note equals 126

Measure one begins at the F-sharp major section, marked tempo giusto. Play measures one through sixteen as written, and skip to measures fifty-seven through seventy-two (second sixteen measures). Then skip to measures one hundred twenty-nine through one hundred forty-four, for the third sixteen measures, and repeat this section to total sixty-four measures. These sixty-four measures may then be repeated as needed. Since these measures are rather spread out, the accompanist is advised to copy or rearrange his score for visual and page-turning purposes.

Loewe (Frederick): "With a Little Bit of Luck" from *My Fair Lady*
⁴/₄, MM half note equals 138

Measure one is where the words begin (use the preceding pickup). Play measures one through eight twice (sixteen measures). Play measures nine through twenty, repeating measures seventeen through twenty (include the pickup to measure seventeen), for another sixteen measures. Play measures twenty-one through twenty-eight twice (include the pickup to measure twenty-one) for a third sixteen-measure phrase. This totals forty-eight measures of music. Repeat and cadence as appropriate.

Minkus: Pas de Deux and Coda from *Don Quixote*
²/₄, MM quarter note equals 136

This is an excellent coda, which is technically very accessible. Use as much music as needed, and repeat as necessary. This music falls into consecutive sixteen-measure sections.

Rodgers (Richard): "Oklahoma" from the musical by the same name
²/₄, MM quarter note equals 138

Begin measure one at the refrain. The refrain is fifty-six measures long. Repeat the last eight measures to total sixty-four measures. Repeat and cadence as appropriate.

Rodgers (Richard): "There is Nothin' Like a Dame" from *South Pacific*
²/₄, MM quarter note equals 138

Measure one begins where the words start (include the pickup to measure one). Play measures one through sixteen. Omit measures seventeen through nineteen. For the second sixteen measures, use measures twenty through thirty-five. This totals thirty-two measures. Repeat and cadence as necessary.

Schumann: "Traumes Wirren" (Restless Dreams) from Fantasiestücke, Op. 12
2/4, MM quarter note equals 138
     Play the first sixteen measures as written. Play measures seventeen through twenty-four twice. Repeat the whole section as necessary.

Tchaikovsky: Russian Dance from *The Nutcracker*
2/4, MM quarter note equals 138
     Play measures one through thirty-two as written. For another thirty-two measures, play measures thirty-three through forty-eight, then play measures forty-nine through fifty-six twice. Repeat this whole section as necessary (sixty-four measures).

Tchaikovsky: Czardas from *Swan Lake*
2/4, MM quarter note equals 126
     Begin at the vivace section of the czardas. Measures one through four are introductory. Use the following sixty-four measures and repeat as necessary.

Tour en l'air

     Tour en l'air is done by male dancers (almost exclusively) in many grand allegro combinations. When this step is practiced alone, the accompanist may use a broad, powerful grand allegro waltz or perhaps another strong 3/4. He may also use a broad, powerful 4/4 with drive and energy. The music must thrust the dancer up into the air.

Brahms: Variations on a Theme by Handel, Op. 24 Var. XXV
4/4, MM quarter note equals 69
     Refer to the section on music for grand battement which describes how to arrange this variation. Those instructions may be applied here.

Glazunov: Var. III from *Raymonda*
2/4, MM quarter note equals 69

Measures one and two are introductory. Use measures three through thirty-four, as written, and cadence where appropriate.

Schubert: Twelve Valses Nobles, Op. 77, D. 969, No. 1
¾, MM dotted half note equals 60

Use measures one through thirty-two as written. Cadence where appropriate.

Schumann: Marche des Davidsbündler Contre les Philistins from Carnaval, Op. 9
¾, MM dotted half note equals 60

Use the first eight measures and repeat. For the second sixteen measures, play measures nine through twenty-four. Cadence where appropriate.

Preparing and Arranging Piano Repertory for Ballet Class

How to Play a Musical Preparation

The first topic to be dealt with in this chapter is the use of musical introductions, or preparations, which are employed to precede the actual music for the various dance exercises and steps. There are basically two classes of musical preparations to be considered: the first is used with slower, smoother combinations, while the second is chiefly for the quicker, sharper combinations.

The type of musical preparation which should be used for the slower, smoother combinations is, in its simplest form, merely two introductory chords. These two introductory chords should be played in the same tempo as that to which the combination will be danced. This preparation is clearer and more helpful if the two chords are broken, or arpeggiated, in a way which will define the rhythmic pulse. In the following pages, several specific examples are given for both the slow, chordal type of preparation and for the quicker, sharper style of preparation.

The preparation which is employed for the brighter, sharper combinations must indicate very clearly the exact pulse and feeling of the music which is to follow. It may consist of either four or eight beats for ²/₄ or ⁴/₄ steps. If the step is extremely fast, eight beats are more desirable, giving the dancers more time in which to prepare. These beats may be simply an ostinato figure or perhaps the closing two or four bars of the piece to be played. In the case of bright waltzes, two or four bars of introduction will be required. If the dancers need more time in which to prepare, then four bars is best. Again, the preparation may be two or four bars of improvised waltz rhythm or perhaps the final two or four bars of the waltz itself. In the cases where a mazurka or a polonaise is used, the same principles apply. Use two or four bars of a characteristic mazurka or polonaise rhythm or perhaps the closing two or four bars of the piece itself, if appropriate.

The following chart divides the various exercises and steps into categories, according to barre and center, and indicates which preparation is generally the more appropriate, the slow, chordal preparation or the faster, ostinato-type preparation. Following the chart are numerous representative examples which demonstrate explicitly what a suitable preparation would be for any given exercise or step. All of the following musical examples are taken from the repertory lists in the preceding chapter, so that the reader may conveniently refer back to them if he desires to do so.

The examples convey the essence of preparations. Obviously, there are many possible variations that may be just as suitable. Introductory chords and arpeggios do not always have to be on the tonic. Any chord progression or passage which clearly leads to the opening harmony of the music is acceptable. The accompanist is encouraged to use his imagination and to employ many rhythmic and harmonic variations of preparations. The only requirement is that they must blend naturally and logically with the music being used for the combination.

Preparations Chart

Slow preparations
(two arpeggiated chords)

BARRE | CENTER
Stretches — Adagio
Pliés — Slow Pirouettes, in Place
Port de Bras — Révérence
Fondus
Développés
Slow Battements Tendus
Ronds de Jambe à Terre

Fast preparations
(ostinato: two or
four bars of music)

BARRE
Fast Battements Tendus
Battements Tendus Dégagés
Pointés
Ronds de Jambe en l'Air
Battements Frappés
Battement sur le Cou-de-Pied
Pas de Cheval
Battements en Cloche
Grand Battements

CENTER
Petit Allegro Steps (²⁄₄ and ¾)
Pirouettes: Quick, in Place,
   and Quick, Moving
Tours en l'Air
Relevés and Sous-Sus
Grand Allegro Steps (²⁄₄ and ¾)

Slow Preparations at the Barre

PLIÉS: Ravel: Waltz No. 2 in G Minor, Valses Nobles et Sentimentales
MM quarter note equals 88

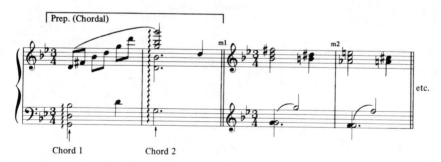

FONDUS: Chopin: Nocturne in F Minor, Op. 55 No. 1
MM quarter note equals 80

RONDS DE JAMBE À TERRE: Bach: Passepied II, Partita in B Minor
(Overture in the French Manner)
MM eighth note equals 104

DÉVELOPPÉS: Brahms: Intermezzo, Op. 117 No. 1
MM eighth note equals 92

Fast Preparations at the Barre

BATTEMENT TENDU DÉGAGÉ: Liszt: Hungarian Rhapsody No. 6
MM quarter note equals 96

BATTEMENT FRAPPÉ: Bach: Bouree II, Partita in B Minor (Overture in the French Manner)
MM half note equals 88

    In this example, the two-measure introduction consists of the last two measures of the first sixteen-measure section. (Remember that this original twelve-measure phrase has measures one through four repeated to make sixteen measures.)

BATTEMENT SUR LE COU-DE-PIED: Schumann: "Wild Rider," from Album for the Young, Op. 68.
MM dotted quarter note equals 126

    In this example, the two-measure introduction consists of the final two measures of the piece.

BATTEMENT EN CLOCHE: Beethoven: Theme, Variations on a Waltz by Diabelli

MM dotted half note equals 69

GRAND BATTEMENT: Brahms: Variations on a Theme by Paganini, Op. 35, Book I, Var. XIII

MM quarter note equals 69

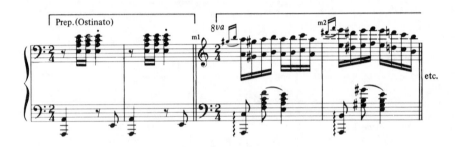

Slow Preparations in the Center

ADAGIO: Brahms: Variations on a Theme by Paganini, Op. 35, Book II, Var. XII.

MM eighth note equals 104.

In this example, the preparation is the final measure of the variation (measure 12).

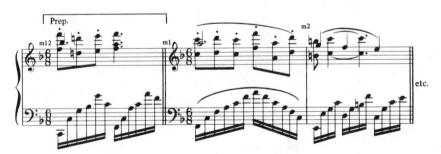

Glazunov: Barcarolle from *The Seasons*. MM eighth note equals 116.

Use the imagination in playing preparations. Do not always just play dominant and tonic chords.

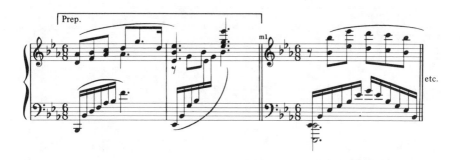

Rachmaninoff: Prelude, Op. 23 No. 5. MM quarter note equals 66.

SLOW PIROUETTE FROM 4TH, 5TH, 2ND. Brahms: Waltz in A-Flat Major, Op. 39 No. 15. MM quarter note equals 126.

Fast Preparations in the Center

PETIT ALLEGRO (²/₄). Grieg: Album Leaf, Op. 12 No. 7. MM quarter note equals 88.

GRAND ALLEGRO WALTZ: Schubert: Twelve Valses Nobles, Op. 77 No. 9. MM dotted half note equals 66.

or:

Schumann: Waltz, Op. 124 No. 4. MM dotted half note equals 66. Here is an inventive preparation.

FOUETTÉ. Minkus: Pas de Deux, Coda from *Don Quixote*. MM quarter note equals 136.

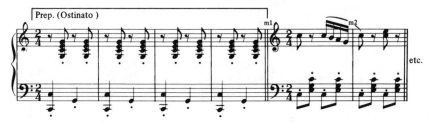

TOUR EN L'AIR: Glazunov: Var. III from *Raymonda*. MM quarter note equals 69.

Other Examples of Preparations

POLONAISE. For a polonaise, use the following standard rhythmic motive for a preparation:

The following is a simple but adequate example of a preparation for a polonaise which is in E major.

Below is a good preparation which might be used for the Polonaise in F-sharp minor, Op. 44, of Chopin. This two-measure preparation precedes the opening phrase, which begins in measure nine.

MAZURKA. For a mazurka, use the following standard rhythmic motive for a preparation:

The following is a simple but adequate example of a preparation for a mazurka which is in F minor.

Below is a good preparation which might be used for the mazurka from Act I of *Coppelia.*

A few other examples of suitable musical preparations are given below, for various hypothetical time and key signatures in different tempos.

Slow ⁴/₄, E Major (chordal). MM quarter note equals 66.

Slow ¾, B-Flat Major (chordal). MM quarter note equals 76.

POLONAISE, A-Flat Major. MM quarter note equals 88.

PETIT ALLEGRO (²/₄), B Major, MM quarter note equals 92.

GRAND ALLEGRO WALTZ, C Major. MM dotted half note equals 66.

Cadences

The ballet accompanist surveying the musical suggestions in the preceding chapter and doing his own research will discover that in arranging music for class he will frequently have to improvise cadences at key spots in the score in order to coincide with the end of dance combinations. These cadences should not sound abrupt, chopped off, or unexpected. They must occur in every case at the ends of musical phrases, after multiples of eight bars. In all of the repertory given in Chapter 3, the accompanist is told specifically where to cadence and is given guidance concerning how to end gracefully in a proper key.

Many kinds of cadences will work. The accompanist must simply remember to make them sound as natural and smooth as possible, within the context of whatever piece is being played. Listed below are several examples of possible cadential solutions, taken from the pieces listed in Chapter 3. In arranging music to fit into even, square phrases, the accompanist will notice that the desired cadential point often occurs at an inconvenient place, and he must be able to formulate a logical ending. In studying the following examples, the accompanist may refer back in each case to the detailed cadential instructions given in the preceding chapter.

PLIÉ: Fauré: Nocturne in E-Flat Major, Op. 36. MM quarter note equals 50.

FONDU: Schumann: "Erinnerung" from Album for the Young, Op. 68. MM quarter note equals 52.

BATTEMENT SUR LE COU-DE-PIED: Chopin: Etude in A Minor, Op. 25 No. 4. MM quarter note equals 132.

Improvised cadence: End of phrase

ADAGIO: Chopin: Etude, Op. 25 No. 5. MM quarter note equals 138.

As written: Desired phrase ending

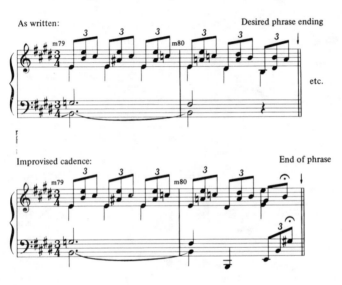

Improvised cadence: End of phrase

PETIT ALLEGRO (²/₄): Czerny: The Art of Finger Dexterity, Op. 740 No. 33. MM dotted quarter note equals 96.

As written: Desired phrase ending

PETIT ALLEGRO (¾): Tchaikovsky: Tempo di Valse from Weihnachten, Op. 37 No. 12. MM dotted half note equals 80.

As written, the phrase which comprises measures twenty-nine through thirty-two is intended to continue on and is not strong enough to be a convincing final cadence. The following change is recommended.

Simplifying Music

The ballet accompanist may frequently discover pieces which have excellent potential for use in the ballet class, but be discouraged by the fact that the music is very difficult technically and might require considerable time to prepare. The accompanist may not have excessive extra time to practice repertory outside the ballet studio. If this is the case, he can often simplify the music so that it is immediately more

playable, without destroying the essential qualities which make it a
good dance piece. The accompanist will also discover, when he is
required to sight-read difficult renditions of ballet scores at short
notice, that he can frequently simplify them without impairing their
effectiveness.

One obvious example is Variation XIII, Book I, of the Paganini
Variations by Brahms. It was previously mentioned in this chapter with
relation to preparations. This variation, which is used for grand battement, has a right-hand melody of rapid sixteenth-note octaves. There
is no reason why the accompanist cannot make this variation more
technically accessible by playing the melody as just one note, rather
than in octaves. The music is somewhat less forceful, but it is still
effective, if the accompanist plays the right hand as strongly as possible.

One may also refer to the Czerny exercise Op. 740 No. 33, an
excerpt of which is given in this chapter under the section dealing with
cadences. Here again is a rapid melody in octaves, which may be
simplified. This exercise must have a light, dancy character, as it is used
for petit allegro, and a preponderance of heavy, badly-played octaves
would not encourage the proper feeling. Of course, if the accompanist
can play octaves well and can render them light enough at the proper
speed, there is no reason to omit them.

As written:

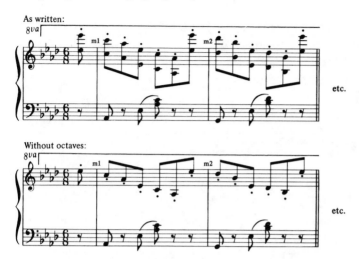

Without octaves:

There are times in the dance class when brilliance and virtuosity are most effective, as long as they do not interfere with the essence of the music. Brilliant playing on a grand scale is particularly inspiring in grand allegro steps, and a well-developed technique is a real asset. But the accompanist cannot play himself to death all of the time, and where it is appropriate, he should not hesitate to cut out of the music unnecessary and encumbering material. The following musical examples contain material which may be clumsy if the tempo becomes too fast and should then be omitted.

BATTEMENT TENDU: Brahms: Variations on a Theme by Handel, Op. 24 Var. I. MM quarter note equals 60.

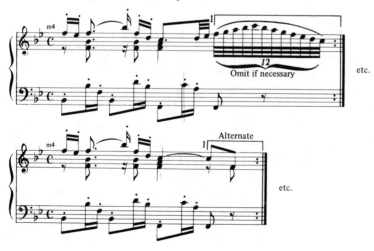

PETIT ALLEGRO (²/₄): Czerny, The Art of Finger Dexterity, Op. 740 No. 35. MM quarter note equals 84.

The rapid triplets may be replaced by more manageable duplets, which are easier to play at fast speeds.

The accompanist should use his own good judgment, based on an understanding of his technical limits, in deciding when to omit material which he considers to be musically nonessential and technically over-demanding.

Arranging, Enriching, and Embellishing Music

The accompanist may frequently want to enrich, embellish, or otherwise arrange music which he uses for the ballet class. In time, this practice becomes natural, instinctive, and spontaneous, as the accompanist learns more and more what kinds of musical textures are helpful and suitable for given steps and combinations. At times, a sparseness of notes and a simple texture can be not only functional but also elegant. At other times, a quality of fullness, weight, or motion can be enhanced if the music is embellished and colored or enriched with more moving tones. A sense of breadth and expansiveness may be thus imparted to pliés or to adagio music. Grand battement music may be given more weight and power. Petit and grand allegro music may be rendered fuller and given more substance. Bass patterns, in particular, may be given more energy and drive by replacing single notes which fall on the downbeat with octaves or chords, or by playing them in a sharper, more accented manner than the score itself would indicate.

The outstanding advantage in being able to arrange music freely is that the same piece may be manipulated to suit many different steps and combinations. This gives the accompanist a tremendous advantage and enables him to stretch his repertory to a very large degree. Much of the repertory in Chapter 3 may be used for a considerable variety of dance steps, often requiring little more than a tempo adjustment and different touch. In other cases, the music might undergo a considerable metamorphosis.

The various examples throughout the remainder of this chapter demonstrate how music may be enriched and embellished and made usable for many different combinations. Musical snobbery and puritanism should be discarded. They are only impediments. The accompanist should consider the following factors: rendering the music fuller and more expansive for the dancer's ear, heightening the expressive effects which are already present in the music, and imbuing the music with greater rhythmic vitality and general danceability. The accompanist should constantly strive to accomplish these things without destroying or vulgarizing the inherent esthetic beauty of a given piece of music. Many of the examples which follow are taken from the repertory lists in Chapter 3. Other examples are entirely new; some are, as written, unsuitable for any ballet combination, but may be arranged so as to be quite effective.

The reader should bear in mind that this chapter is not intended in any way to be a thorough treatment of the techniques of improvisation. It is hoped, however, that it will at least stimulate the thinking and the imagination of the accompanist and enable him to realize that he has a tremendous amount of freedom to use music in any way which will render it adaptable for his accompanying purposes. If he uses this freedom, it will help him in locating and employing material, in avoiding ruts in his musical thinking, and in sharpening his concepts of what music best compliments and supports the work of the dancers.

The examples are arranged alphabetically by composer. They are brief, but give the accompanist, in each case, a clear idea as to the trend to follow. Most examples are four measures long; others are two or eight measures, where appropriate.

Bach: Menuet II, Partita in B-Flat Major.
Plié: MM quarter note equals 88.

As is the case with much traditional piano repertory when it is used for ballet class, the tempo may be greatly altered. When the above menuet is used for slow pliés, it is played a great deal slower than the original tempo. Thus, the following alteration is very appropriate, as it helps to sustain the music at a considerably diminished tempo.

Bach: Bouree II, Partita in B Minor (Overture in the French Manner)

Played as written, this movement was listed as well-suited for battement tendu dégagé. Because of its thin texture, it would not be so suitable for a slower combination. The example given below shows how the material might be modified and enriched for a slower combination such as pas de cheval.

Battement tendu dégagé: MM half note equals 88.

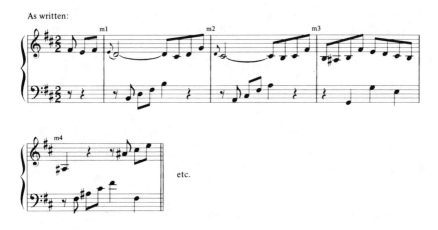

Arranged for pas de cheval: MM half note equals 60.

Beethoven: Third Movement from Sonata, Op. 31 No. 2.

As written, the opening of this movement is a logical sixteen-measure phrase which, when suitably arranged, would be quite effective for battement frappé. The meter is changed from a ³⁄₈ to a ²⁄₄. Sixteen measures of the original equals eight measures in the arranged example.

As written: MM dotted quarter note equals 69.

Arranged for battement frappé: MM quarter note equals 88.

Brahms: Variations on a Theme by Paganini, Op. 35, Book I, Var. XI.

As written, this piece was suggested for fondus. This variation might be modified in a number of ways for other combinations. Two possibilities are suggested below, one for ronds de jambe, the other for battement frappé. Thus, this material undergoes a change in texture, tempo, and meter.

Fondu: MM eighth note equals 50.

Arranged for ronds de jambe à terre: MM eighth note equals 112.

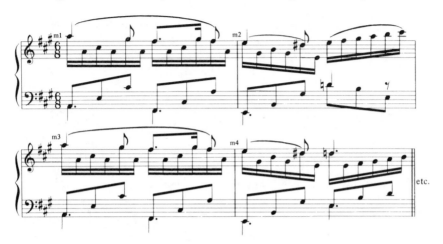

Arranged for battement frappé: MM quarter note equals 88.

Chopin: Etude, Op. 25 No. 4

As written, this etude was suggested for battement sur le cou-de-pied. Below are two arranged versions. The first is for a moderate battement tendu. In this slower version, the bass is made more substantial, and the right hand is enriched with moving notes. The second arranged version is for battement en cloche. The texture is modified, and the meter is changed to a swinging ⁶⁄₈ waltz feeling.

Battement sur le cou-de-pied: MM quarter note equals 132.

Arranged for moderate battement tendu: MM quarter note equals 60.

Arranged for battement en cloche: MM dotted quarter note equals 66.

 The reader will note that in the example below, one measure of music is equivalent to one half measure of music in the original etude. In other words, the harmonic rhythm of the following example is half as fast as in the original music.

Chopin: Prelude in C Major, Op. 28 No. 1

    This prelude is not really appropriate for any ballet class combination, as written. However, the examples which follow demonstrate that it can be arranged so as to be excellent for at least two combinations.

As written: MM eighth note equals 176.

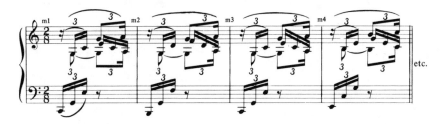

Arranged for pointés: MM eighth note equals 132.

    The rhythm is made sharper and more defined by rewriting the bass in the fashion of a typical left-hand accompaniment.

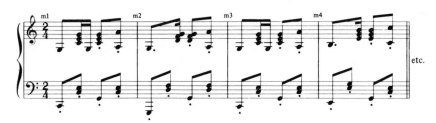

Arranged for ronds de jambe à terre: MM quarter note equals 116.

    The meter is changed to a flowing ¾ and the texture is appropriately rewritten. The harmony is unaltered.

Chopin: Nocturne, Op. 55 No. 1

The combination for which this piece was originally intended is fondu. With minor changes, it can be made into good music for faster ²⁄₄ combinations, both at the barre and in the center. The example which follows is for petit allegro ²⁄₄.

Fondu: MM quarter note equals 80.

Arranged for petit allegro (²⁄₄): MM quarter note equals 88.

Delibes: Mazurka from Act I of *Coppelia*

This piece is listed under pas de basque (grand allegro ¾). The example given below suggests how one may convert this mazurka into a polonaise, by applying some minor rhythmic alterations. It is on occasion very advantageous to be able to convert a mazurka into a polonaise, for example, when a mazurka tempo becomes too draggy and bogged down.

Grand allegro (¾): MM quarter note equals 104.

Arranged for polonaise: MM quarter note equals 84.

Dvořák: Slavonic Dance No. 2

This piece was originally listed under petit allegro ²⁄₄. The following example shows this piece arranged in a ⁶⁄₈ to be suitable for ronds de jambe. It could have just as easily been arranged in ¾, but was done in a ⁶⁄₈ to keep the harmonic rhythm the same as in the original. A ¾ would mean eight measures for every four measures of the original. With a ⁶⁄₈, the number of measures remains the same.

Petit allegro (²⁄₄): MM quarter note equals 92.

Arranged for ronds de jambe à terre: MM dotted quarter note equals 116.

etc.

Fauré: Theme from Theme and Variations, Op. 73

Played as written, this theme is suggested for grand battement. Two excellent examples follow, which are rhythmically modified to render them effective for a polonaise and a développé, respectively. Notice that in the first arrangement, for a polonaise, the harmonic rhythm in each measure is half as fast as the original. In the second arrangement, for a slow waltz, the harmonic rhythm is even slower— only one-fourth as fast as the original example.

Grand battement: MM quarter note equals 60.

etc.

Arranged for a polonaise: MM quarter note equals 88.

Arranged for développé: MM quarter note equals 96.

Granados: Valses Poeticos, No. 1

This waltz, suggested as written for ronds de jambe à terre, would make an excellent, bright ²/₄ for battement sur le cou-de-pied. It requires minor changes, as shown below.

Ronds de jambe à terre: MM quarter note equals 116.

Arranged for battement sur le cou-de-pied: MM quarter note equals 132.

Granados: Valses Poeticos, No. 2

As written, this waltz was suggested for slow pirouettes from 4th, 5th, and 2nd. With skillful enrichment and embellishment, this waltz would make a rather nice adagio piece, as the example which follows demonstrates.

Slow Pirouettes from 4th, 5th, and 2nd: MM quarter note equals 138.

Arranged for adagio: MM quarter note equals 112.

Grieg: Wedding-Day at Troldhaugen, Op. 65 No. 6

As written, this piece was suggested for grand battement. The arranged version below is in a ⁶⁄₈ meter and has a swinging quality which would be very well suited for battement en cloche.

Grand battement: MM half note equals 60.

As written:

As arranged for battement en cloche: MM dotted quarter note equals 63.

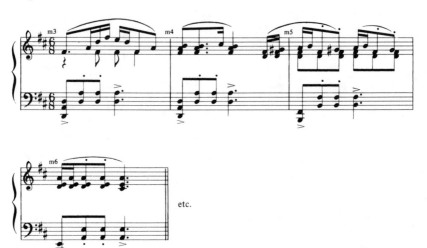

Mozart: Second Movement, Sonata in F Major, K. 332

As written, this slow movement was suggested for adagio. It would also make a nice bright ²/₄ with skillful handling.

Adagio: MM eighth note equals 76.

As arranged for battement tendu: MM quarter note equals 60.

Rachmaninoff: Variations on a Theme of Corelli, Op. 42 Var. IV

This piece was originally suggested for développés. It will also make an excellent arrangement for grand battement, when written into a powerful ²⁄₄ style.

Développé: MM quarter note equals 88.

Arranged for grand battement: MM quarter note equals 69.

Schubert: Twelve Valses Nobles, Op. 77, D. 969, No. 1

As written, this waltz is suggested for battement en cloche. When the meter is changed to ⁴⁄₄, it is suitable for tour en l'air (or grand battement). Note the example given below.

Battement en cloche: MM dotted half note equals 66.

Arranged for tour en l'air: MM half note equals 69.

Schubert: Twelve Valses Nobles, Op. 77, D. 969, No. 4

    As written, this waltz was suggested for grand allegro ¾. It may be easily arranged so as to be a most suitable piece for petit allegro ²⁄₄ or for various tendu combinations at the barre.

Grand allegro (¾): MM dotted half note equals 69.

Arranged for petit allegro: MM half note equals 84.

Schumann: Promenade from Carnaval, Op. 9

This piece, as written, was suggested for slow pirouettes from 4th, 5th, and 2nd. It might be arranged, as in the following example, for battement tendu (quick).

Slow pirouettes from 4th, 5th, and 2nd: MM quarter note equals 138.

As arranged for battement tendu (quick): MM quarter note equals 60.

Schumann: Valse Allemande from Carnaval, Op. 9

As written, this waltz was suggested for grand allegro ¾. Like the preceding Schumann example, this movement would make a fine ²⁄₄, perhaps for battement frappé.

Grand allegro (¾): MM dotted half note equals 63.

As arranged for battement frappé: MM half note equals 88.

Schumann: Waltz, Op. 124 No. 4.

This piece was listed under grand allegro ¾. The example below demonstrates how the texture may be enriched somewhat in order to render the music fuller and more powerful. The characteristic grand allegro waltz rhythm in the right hand of measure four, as written, is generally more helpful in the odd-numbered measures, as was discussed earlier. Note the following example and the rhythmic alternatives offered in the starred measures.

Grand allegro (¾): MM dotted half note equals 66.

etc.

etc.

Schumann: Novellette, Op. 21 No. 2

This piece, not taken from the repertory lists in Chapter 3, is not exactly suitable for any combination as written. Arranged, however, it could be very usable in a number of contexts. The following examples illustrate this and demonstrate graphically that music should not be disregarded as unusable for ballet class simply because, as written, it is not immediately functional. The accompanist should always examine potential ballet material with an open mind and an active imagination. He can thus greatly expand and develop his dance repertory, both in terms of quantity and style.

The most readily adaptable material in the Schumann Novellette is measures one through sixteen. The original tempo marking is MM quarter note equals 152. The following three examples alter markedly the tempo, meter, and texture of the original material, while preserv-

ing the general melodic contour. The first four measures are reproduced below.

As written: MM quarter note equals 152.

Arranged for battement tendu degagé: MM quarter note equals 88.

Arranged for ronds de jambe à terre: MM quarter note equals 116.

Arranged for grand allegro (¾): MM dotted half note equals 63.
    Like the above example, this arrangement has been changed to a

triple meter and has been cast in the style of a typical grand allegro waltz.

Scriabin: Etude in E Major, Op. 8 No. 5

This etude, as written, is listed under ronds de jambe en l'air. The example given below, of the first two measures, is sufficient to demonstrate that this material may be arranged to make a very lovely adagio. One beat of the original material is equivalent to one ¾ measure of the arranged material.

Ronds de jambe en l'air: MM half note equals 50.

Arranged for adagio: MM quarter note equals 104.

Since the harmonic rhythm of the adagio is only one quarter as fast per measure as the original material, the first four measures of the original material would equal sixteen measures of adagio music.

Tchaikovsky: Chanson Triste, Op. 40 No. 2

As written, this piece is listed under ronds de jambe en l'air. Two examples of arrangements follow. The first example renders the material as a sharp ²⁄₄, suitable for bright combinations like battement frappé. The second example converts the material into a smooth waltz, suitable for ronds de jambe à terre.

Ronds de jambe en l'air: MM half note equals 50.

Arranged for battement frappé: MM quarter note equals 88.

Arranged for ronds de jambe à terre: MM quarter note equals 116.

In the following example, the harmonic rhythm of each measure is again changed. One measure of the original material equals two measures of waltz in the arranged version.

Tchaikovsky: Schneeglöckchen, Op. 37 No. 4

This piece was originally suggested for ronds de jambe à terre. The example given below converts the original material to an adagio, by enriching and embellishing it.

Ronds de jambe à terre: MM eighth note equals 116.

Arranged for adagio: MM eighth note equals 100.

Smooth, sustained

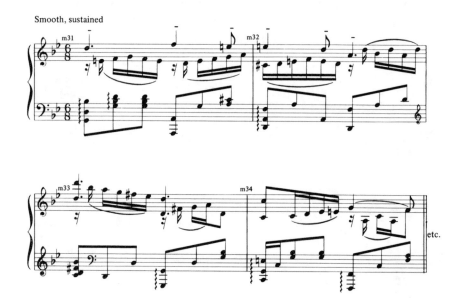

Ballet-Related Accompanying outside the Technique Class

The accompanist who plays for the ballet will in many cases do other ballet-related accompanying outside of the technique class. This work may include accompanying for pointe classes, ballet repertory classes and rehearsals, adagio (partnering) classes, and national character dance classes. Each deals with a special aspect of ballet, and a professional dancer will be thoroughly trained in each area. In doing the accompanying work mentioned above, the accompanist may want to make some special preparations.

Pointe Class

Pointe work involves female dancers only. This type of work is done while wearing hard-toed pointe shoes, which enable the dancer to balance on the ends of the toes. Pointe work is very demanding and often painful. It requires years of proper training and conditioning in order to be done without discomfort or injury to the dancer. The female dancers may wear their pointe shoes during all or part of technique class, depending on the conditioning and ability of the individual. Training the dancers to balance properly and strengthening their feet and ankles is of central importance in pointe work. The accompanist will notice that correctness of approach is heavily stressed and that the rising steps discussed earlier (relevés and sous-sus) are basic to pointe work (indeed, to all dancing).

In the pointe class, there may or may not be some barre work to warm up the dancers' feet. It is usually better for the dancer if she has had ample opportunity to become thoroughly warmed up before attempting pointe work (it is helpful if she has taken a technique class beforehand). After the barre work (which may include many of the traditional combinations used in barre work for technique class—pliés, ronds de jambes, etc.), the dancers proceed to the center work. The material covered in pointe class may seem less established and organized than in the technique class and will vary from session to session. After playing for pointe class several times, the accompanist will have a better grasp of the situation and will know in a general way what to expect.

Much of the literature which the accompanist uses for technique class may be employed in the pointe class, if certain considerations are borne in mind. Most music for pointe class demands an especially light, uplifting quality. Music which is heavy, weighty, or lugubrious is generally not suitable. The majority of ²/₄'s used should be played with a strong upbeat and should have a bright, staccato quality in order to underscore the sharp, precise movements of the dancers. The accompanist should have available a number of waltzes with a light, running character, for bourées and other steps. In other words, the accompanist's approach to pointe work should be characterized by a quality of lightness and clarity, supported by a rhythmic pulse which is bright and well accented.

Adagio (Partnering) Class

Adagio classes train the dance student to work with other dancers. Although more than two dancers may sometimes work together, adagio work is usually done with one partner. Thus, each female dancer is paired off with a male dancer, and their work together trains them in the various aspects of pas de deux. Not all of the work in pas de deux is of an adagio nature, by any means, although much of it is. The partners will learn how to waltz together, how to perform mazurkas and polonaises and a wide variety of many other combinations and styles.

The accompanist, accordingly, will use a wide range of musical styles for adagio classes. If he comes equipped with the same scope and quality of music which he should be using for technique classes, he should find himself well-prepared. In particular, he should provide himself with a plentiful repertory of adagios and with waltzes of all varieties. Often, adagio work will require some specific piece of music from the ballet repertory, in which case the accompanist will be confronted with various piano reductions from ballets, which range in readability and difficulty from moderate to nearly impossible. Thus, the accompanist should either get hold of scores ahead of time and do some preparation, or he should be strong in sight-reading. Outside of occasional sight-reading, however, he should not encounter any special difficulties with adagio accompanying. It demands the same standards of alertness and musicality which are necessary for ballet accompanying in general.

Repertory Class

The purpose of repertory classes is to teach the dancers the various choreographies of established ballet literature. Corps de ballet work is emphasized. The dancers perform together in groups of varying size, learning dance steps, concentrating on working as an organized, cooperating unit, while becoming familiar with traditional ballet works.

It is in the repertory class that the accompanist must truly be a skillful sight-reader. As mentioned, many ballet reductions are extremely difficult to read at sight. Some hardly seem like reductions at all, and their arrangers seem determined to cram in everything from the original orchestra score. Of course, the reading is somewhat easier to handle if the accompanist has at least some familiarity with the sound of the music. (It is easier to fake.) Whether the accompanist does some outside preparation (advisable for poor sight-readers) or sight-reads the score during class, he will often find it helpful, even necessary, to determine what is of primary importance in the score and what is nonessential material. He should first strive to communicate the essential melodic, harmonic, and rhythmic content of the score, and from that point may add whatever else he can handle. Once he has grasped the essence of the music, he will find it much easier to add other embellishing and enriching material.

Often, the accompanist will discover that the score does not include tempo variations and changes which the dancers may require. Various musical accommodations will be asked of him, and he should either note them down or bear them in mind from rehearsal to rehearsal. It will save much time in rehearsals if he can also get a general idea of what choreography goes with what music. The choreographer will not have to take the time to wade through all of the music with the accompanist to show him where the dancers are starting.

The dancers depend on the accompanist's ability to reproduce accurately the music in all of its aspects from one rehearsal to another. The accompanist who can remember the kinds of information mentioned above will be a great help to the teacher or choreographer. He will be able to remind them of the various counts and measure numbers which go with different steps and offer much support in accurately retaining correct tempos, pauses, and other musical data. These abilities, which a good accompanist should possess, develop gradually with time and experience, as he does more repertory and rehearsal work.

Character Class

In character class, the dancers learn the various steps which comprise the national character and folk dances of different countries. A thorough training in character work is essential to the aspiring professional dancer, since much corps work is made up of character dances, including the mazurka, tarantella, czardas, and many others. Since most dancers start out in the corps de ballet of dance companies, they had better be proficient in character dance if they expect to be hired and to keep their jobs.

As in repertory work, some of the material which the accompanist will be required to play will come from the traditional ballet scores, as they contain a plentiful assortment of character music. Much of the class time, however, will be used in teaching and drilling the dancers in basic character steps at the barre and in the center. The accompanist who plays for character classes will gradually acquire some knowledge as to the essential nature of various character steps. He should acquire an adequate collection of character music in many styles, and with experience should be able to improvise in different styles which approximate the various character idioms. Many instructors own their own character music, which they will make available for the accompanist's use. Otherwise, there are collections available which the accompanist may purchase.

Outside of the basic repertory differences, there should not be any particular problems for an experienced dance accompanist in playing for character classes. Following is an assortment of character dances, representative of some of the major countries, which might be taught in character classes. The list is by no means complete, but will familiarize the accompanist with the tempo and quality of some of the major character dances.

Character Chart

AUSTRIA

Schuhplattler	Moderate ¾
Ländler	Moderate ¾

CZECHOSLOVAKIA

Janoshka	Slow ²/₄
Kalamajka	Light ²/₄

ENGLAND

Morris Dance	Steady ⁴/₄
Sailor's Hornpipe	Bright ²/₄

FRANCE

Bourée	Slow ¾
Farandole	Quick ⁶/₈
Gavotte	Bright ⁴/₄
Quadrille	Moderate ²/₄

GREECE

Syrto	Slow ⁴/₄, followed by fast ²/₄

HUNGARY

Czardas	Slow ⁴/₄, followed by fast ²/₄

IRELAND

Jig	Quick ⁶/₈

ITALY

Tarantella	Fast ⁶/₈

POLAND

Krakoviak	Fast 4/4
Mazurka	Moderate 3/4
Polonaise	Stately 3/4

RUSSIA

Gopak	Fast 2/4
Khorovod	Stately 2/4
Troika	Fast 2/4

SCOTLAND

Fling	Steady 4/4
Reel	Quick 4/4
Sword Dance	Steady 4/4

SPAIN

Jota	Quick 3/8
Tango	Moderate 2/4

SWEDEN

Daldans	Moderate 3/4

YUGOSLAVIA

Kolo	Moderate 2/4

Last Thoughts:
Special Problems for
the Accompanist

Muscular Difficulties

Some difficulties which can occur in connection with ballet accompanying relate specifically to the accompanist and will be problems
only to him. They do not affect the dancers, and indeed the dancers will
generally be unaware of the accompanist's personal professional
hazards, even though they can be significantly troublesome for him.

Some dance accompanists are particulary susceptible to muscular
problems. Accompanying may either create the problem, or it may
aggravate an already existing one. Tendonitis may be a threat to ballet
accompanists, particularly for those who, as pianists, are naturally
somewhat tense and stiff in their approach to playing. Until he is truly
secure and comfortable with ballet accompanying (wich may take a year
or so), the ballet accompanist will most likely find himself at times
under some degree of mental tension, caused by the fact that he is
constantly vulnerable to scrutiny and criticism from the instructor and
from the dancers. He is always on the spot and much is demanded of
him, particularly if the instructor is highly professional. Many instructors and dancers are quite uninhibited when it comes to offering
criticism to the accompanist, and this, quite naturally, may cause some
anxiety which will reflect in his physical approach to playing the piano.
For this reason, the accompanist should make every effort to remain as
relaxed as possible. Tension interferes with proper working of the

muscles and can damage the hands and wrists. An accompanist is particularly vulnerable if he is playing and practicing a great deal on his own time, besides doing accompanying work. A professional dance pianist may accompany between twenty and thirty hours per week, which can be a great strain. The author speaks from much personal experience in this area.

These potential dangers can generally be circumnavigated by the proper measures. If the ballet accompanist has acquired a solid, correct piano technique and remains relaxed, while being careful not to form bad playing habits, he is far less apt to incur muscular complications. There are some other factors to consider, however, and they will be taken up in the following discussion. They are particularly pertinent in the case of the pianist who tends to be somewhat aggressive and tight in his approach to piano playing.

Frequent Starting and Stopping

This discussion is applicable to both barre and center work. On occasions the accompanist may sit at the piano for several minutes between combinations without playing. During this time the instructor may be giving detailed corrections to the dancers or explaining a combination (and it is deadly impolite to practice while the instructor is talking). After sitting idle for some time, the accompanist must take care that he does not incur strain or damage his hands when resuming his accompanying. This warning is particularly applicable in cases where the next combination is very fast or demanding. Let the pianist who is skeptical about this beware! It can happen.

A cold studio is hazardous to the dancers. It should be comfortably warm, so as not to cramp cold muscles. However, studios are occasionally rather poorly heated and sometimes drafty. If the accompanist has a significant problem in keeping his hands warm, an excellent solution is to take an old pair of gloves (preferably knit) and cut off the ends of the fingers, so that when they are worn, about half the length of the fingers protrudes, unencumbered. These the pianist may wear while he is accompanying, at least until the muscles in his hands and wrists are warm. They should not be worn all the time, because one becomes unduly dependent on them. Analogously, many dancers develop an unhealthy dependence on leg and ankle warmers and similar apparel, from wearing them when it is really unnecessary.

Long Combinations

Earlier in the text it was stated that the accompanist may sometimes play for long periods of time without pause or rest (up to ten or fifteen minutes in more extreme cases), particularly for grand allegro combinations in the center, in which the dancers go in single file or in groups one after the other across the room. If the accompanist is playing a huge symphonic-style waltz or a wild galop, he can become totally exhausted, mentally and physically. Even in demanding, large-scale virtuoso piano pieces, the composer provides periods of physical and emotional repose. This will not be the case in much grand allegro work. The dancers have an opportunity to rest after their individual group is finished, while the accompanist must keep right on playing for the succeeding groups of dancers. Dancers, and sometimes instructors, tend to forget this. The instructor who works the accompanist unfairly without giving him occasional rest is inexcusably inconsiderate and rude. In such cases, where the accompanist is taken advantage of, he is totally justified in reminding the instructor of his needs. The accompanist, as well as the dancers, deserves an occasional rest. If he is doing his job properly, he will probably need one.

Producing a Full Sound and Thinking Chordally

Muscular strain or aggravation of previous muscular problems may occur as the result of one or two other factors which are related to ballet accompaniment. One is the frequent need to produce very full and massive sounds and textures for an extended period (as in grand allegro work), and the other is the tendency on the part of the accompanist to think and play chordally (as opposed to being more melodically oriented). The need to produce large sounds for support in certain combinations is obvious and has already been discussed to some extent in the section dealing with long combinations. It will suffice here to state that when this style of accompanying is demanded, the accompanist's approach should be a correct one. To avoid injury, he should remain relaxed throughout the wrists and arms and should use the weight of the arm in producing large sounds. If he finds himself working beyond his limit and playing unnaturally, then the studio needs a better piano or the dancers are expecting too much.

Presumably, the accompanist possesses or is developing some

ability to improvise and to take pieces of existing music and embellish them, thickening and enriching them so that they offer full support for the dance movements. To do this, the accompanist must possess some knowledge of music theory and harmony, either instinctively or objectively. He must analyze his music from a triadic, chordal context to understand its harmonic content, and from that improvise his own embellished chords, textures, and melodies. In thinking chordally, he must not degenerate into being aware of chords and rhythm only. He must project convincing melodies and phrases.

Most dancers will say that the shape of the musical phrase and the quality of the melody are important for them, and that music which is rhythmic only is deadening. This applies to all combinations, and particularly to pliés, port de bras, adagios, waltzes, and other lyrical, flowing combinations. It may not be as crucial for a fast tendu combination at the barre. Although the above discussion might well fit into the context of the chapter which deals specifically with ballet repertory and how to play it, it is very applicable here for the following reason. Thinking and playing in a predominantly chordal fashion tends to work only the wrists and arms, not the fingers. Therefore, for physiological as well as esthetic reasons, it is most important that the accompanist does not neglect the melodic aspect of his improvisation. To do so may mean, particularly over a period of time, loss of proper technique, weakened fingers, and overworked wrists. This leads to tendonitis. It is helpful, of course, if the accompanist has time to practice properly away from the dance studio. Wrong habits must be avoided. They are physically harmful to the accompanist and may erode a balanced sense of musicality which is important to maintain, in both the musician and the dancer.

Musical Ethics: Ballet Accompanying
Versus Solo Playing

In comparing ballet accompanying to solo playing, one finds that in many ways the pianist may employ the same conceptual approach to both areas. On the other hand, some fundamental distinctions must be made: each discipline has its own peculiarities and must be dealt with accordingly.

The pianist should never sacrifice his basic musicality. However, he will never be comfortable in accompanying for dance if he insists on being what some call a musical "purist." The reader may think back to the chapter which deals extensively with the arrangement of traditional piano pieces for the purpose of making them more suitable for ballet accompaniment. Therein are found many examples, suggestions, and techniques for arranging music for ballet combinations. A piece of music can undergo a considerable metamorphosis before it is suitable for the dance class. To be a good ballet accompanist one must do a great deal of this kind of work, and hopefully the pianist will find this an enjoyable challenge. If he finds that this kind of experimentation offends his tastes, he should not play for the ballet.

The arrangement of traditional piano music for dance work should be relegated to the same category as improvisation. Each provides the opportunity for new and varied musical expression, freedom, and growth. Each is a challenge to the imagination. A creative imagination is absolutely essential for such work. Playing the piano in a freer, more spontaneous fashion is an excellent way to offset a tendency to become musically stiff and inflexible from sitting alone in a practice room day after day, memorizing and practicing traditional repertory like a computer. In accompanying the dance, the pianist opens himself up to a whole new area of artistic expression and discipline. Musically, he will grow and expand through this work, if he approaches it with adequate preparation and knowledge and regards it as an artistic discipline worthy of his best effort.

Index of Steps